W9-BIQ-351

06/24

STAND PRICE
$ 5.00

AN AMERICAN DIARY

BARBARA LEIGH SMITH BODICHON

AN AMERICAN DIARY
1857-8

EDITED FROM THE MANUSCRIPT BY

JOSEPH W. REED Jr

ROUTLEDGE & KEGAN PAUL
LONDON

First published 1972
by Routledge and Kegan Paul Ltd
Broadway House,
68–74 Carter Lane,
London, EC4V 5EL

Printed in Great Britain by
Cox & Wyman Ltd, London, Fakenham and Reading

No part of this book may be reproduced in
any form without the permission from the
publisher, except for the quotation of
brief passages in criticism

ISBN 0 7100 7330 5

CONTENTS

ILLUSTRATIONS

ACKNOWLEDGMENTS

The text of the journal is a series of about sixty letters to various correspondents, comprising seventy-three leaves of various sizes. The manuscript was acquired by the Yale University Library in 1954 by purchase from Library Associates Funds, and is published here by its permission and the kind consent of the widow of Philip Leigh Smith, Madame Bodichon's nephew and legal heir. The Beinecke also granted permission to publish passages from the Chapman-Bodichon letters in the Introduction. Ellen Gates D'Oench has prepared the index. My thanks are due to Robert F. Lucid, for his knowledge of Boston in the fifties; to Mrs John F. Lyle and Miss Lenore Jones of the Historic Mobile Preservation Society; to Laura D. S. Harrell of the Mississippi Department of Archives and History in Jackson; to Miss Grace Bacon, Mrs Janette Boothby, Miss Sylvia Joan Jurale and Sister M. Ian, S.S.N.D., of the Wesleyan libraries; to Miss Marjorie Wynne of the Beinecke; to Mrs Anne Fremantle and Hilary Rubinstein; to my colleagues George R. Creeger and Jeffrey E. Butler; and to John Peyton Crigler, Wesleyan 1969, David Ouimette, 1970, John E. Thurner, 1972, Stephen J. Voorhies, 1971 and Jeffrey Wohkittel, 1969, research assistants. Work on this book was assisted by Wesleyan faculty research grants and by the Work-Study Program of the Office of Economic Opportunity which supported a portion of the research assistance.

Middletown, Connecticut

CHAPTER 1

THE ENGLISH VISITORS,
FROM
DICKENS TO TROLLOPE
1841 – 1861

We know that there is a vast continent across the Atlantic, first discovered by a Genoese sailing under the Spanish flag, and that for many years past it has swallowed up thousands of the hardiest of our population. Although our feelings are not particularly fraternal, we give the people . . . the national cognomen of 'Brother Jonathan', while we name individuals 'Yankees'. We know that they are famous for smoking, spitting, 'gouging', and bowie-knives – for monster hotels, steamboat explosions, railway collisions, and repudiated debts. It is believed also that this nation is renowned for keeping three millions of Africans in slavery – for wooden nutmegs, paper money, and 'fillibuster' expeditions . . . I went to the States with that amount of prejudice which seems the birthright of every English person, but I found that . . . these prejudices gradually melted away. I found much which is worthy of commendation, even of imitation: that there is much which is very reprehensible, is not to be wondered at in a country which for years has been made . . . a refuge for those who have 'left their country for their country's good' – a receptacle for the barbarous, the degraded, and the vicious of all other nations (Bishop, 2–3).

The professional English visitor to the States in the 1840s and 1850s came with hopes and expectations mixed: either he expected a visit to the Dark Continent and certain savage tribes and hoped for a trip to Utopia, or vice versa. On the one hand his American cousins had moved physically farther from civilization, but on the other hand the move had given them the advantage of a fresh start on society. The city mice had to divide their time between sneering at and envying the country mice. England at mid-century, in the midst of reform and free-trade agitation, expansion in India and adventure in the Crimea, made America look to some Englishmen like the simplicity of the Golden Age. The eighteenth century's curiosity about the expanding world which had made exotic travel accounts of far-off Pacific and Asian ventures so appealing had given way in the nineteenth century to doubts and misgivings about the right workings of the orderly, civilized societies at home. The old travellers among the savages offered encouragement to England by contrast; mid-century travel in the States aimed more at improvement by comparison. Perhaps there were clues here for the repair of an overcomplicated societal system.

The spectacle of a people founding a home, and designing a constitution, in the remoteness of the West, is one which abounds in interest, not alone in relation to the development of wealth, but in the establishing of all the institutions and habits of the people. It was obviously their design, in forming a community, to escape as far as possible from the errors which had caused the expulsion of the British portion of them from their native land ... Democracy found favour in every department (Ashworth, 181).

A written constitution, soi-disant universal suffrage, unfettered free enterprise and an expanding usable land-mass within its continental borders all gave the States an openness which was inescapably inviting. But at the same time this was the people of the monster hotels and the wooden nutmegs – savages, and rather cocky savages, too.

'These western cocks have crowed loudly,' we said, 'too loudly for the comfort of those who live after all at no such great distance from them. It is well that their combs should be clipped ... It might have gone so far that the clipping would become a work necessarily to be done from without' (Trollope, 6–7).

Hope and expectation and sneer and envy mixed, the traveller braved the journey into alien theory and philosophy. But beyond the theoretical there were some very tangible tourist appeals for the traveller-journalist: a landscape absolutely chock-a-block with sublime views, offering all sorts of new kinds of ferns and rocks, a glimpse of wilderness, perhaps even some not-impossible hotels. For the visitor it was the best of several worlds: things to see, observations to be published and perhaps even some good for society.

To impose the format of tourism on the journal-writers is not entirely fair to the seriousness of their concerns or to the eventual impact of their books. But the tourist quality of the journals themselves is inescapable when one has read twenty or so of them (between 1841 and 1861). Contemporary chic of certain social issues enforced a rather rigid itinerary, a kind of Cook's Tour of the essential sights of the New World. There was an accepted route (the East, the South and maybe the West as far as Ohio at a slightly higher cost), necessary

views (Niagara, Boston, the Mississippi), recurrent comment-
ary on accommodations and conveyance (an almost universal
characteristic of the English traveller is the rather chummy
assumption that all of Britain would shortly come across the
waters, too, and would need some travel tips), conversation
with various kinds and conditions of the citizenry, a large dose
of myth, a small taste of literature and always, looming over
all, a great theme, the corpse at the feast, the skeleton in the
national closet, or (for the pro-slavery group) the endless
project of correcting Mrs Stowe's falsehoods – honest-to-God
slavery taking place before their very eyes.

The general pattern was to land in Boston – taking the
Utopia first was not necessarily thought of as sweet before
meat – proceed down the coast (unless the traveller couldn't
wait to catch Niagara Falls) through New York, Philadelphia, Baltimore, Washington, where a pause in its carefully
planned and essentially empty streets was generally seen as a
last gasp of civilization before plunging into the South and the
'institution'. Rail went only part of the way, through Richmond, thence by various steamers to Charleston, Savannah,
around Florida (a stopping place for only the most dedicated
amateur naturalist or geologist), to New Orleans. Here was
the staging point for the trip up the Mississippi (Natchez,
Vicksburg, Memphis) to St Louis or if the tourist was to go
farther, the Gateway to the West; thence back overland to
New York or Boston and a chance to collect some summary
general observations before heading home.

Boston was not just the home base of convenience for trans-
atlantic crossings. It was also the terminus for the strongest
link between England and America: the intellectual exchange
of the Abolitionist-Transcendentalist-Unitarian-Women's
Rights Axis. For a race determined to hearken no more to the
Courtly Muses of Europe, a remarkable number had been
over to have a look, and Boston, the nation's intellectual
capital, bore the mark of what they had liked. It was an
intellectually concentrated London across the Waters. A visit
to Bronson Alcott's salon, Lowell's or Whittier's home (not
Thoreau's Walden as yet) and one of the great halls to hear a
Channing, a Phillips or Emerson lecture the Gospel of the
New Age were all high spots. Some, like Madame Bodichon,

took to the lectures as a cat takes to milk; Trollope was more dubious:

> A great crowd was collected to hear him. I suppose there were some three thousand persons in the room. I confess that when he took his place before us my prejudices were against him . . . I fancied what might be said on such a subject [war] as to that overlauded star-spangled banner, and how the star-spangled flag would look when wrapped in a mist of mystic Platonism (Trollope, 221).

But even he was struck with the simplicity and directness of the address, even if he remained unconvinced that the lecture could replace church and university at once.

> The men and women of Boston could no more do without their lectures, than those of Paris could do without their theatres. It is the decorous diversion of the best ordered of her citizens. The fast young men go to clubs, and the fast young women to dances, as fast young men and women do in other places that are wicked; but lecturing is the favourite diversion of the steady-minded Bostonian. After all, I do not know that the result is very good. It does not seem that much will be gained by such lectures on either side of the Atlantic, – except that respectable killing of an evening which might otherwise be killed less respectably. It is but an industrious idleness, an attempt at a royal road to information, that habit of attending lectures . . . It is attractive, that idea of being studious without any of the labour of study; but I fear it is illusive (Trollope, 222).

There were some other, perhaps less expected, musts. Laura Bridgman, the amazing deaf-and-blind girl became at Dickens's lead (and by virtue of some of his purplest prose) a sight not to be missed.

> There she was before me; built up, as it were, in a marble cell, impervious to any ray of light, or particle of sound; with her poor white hand peeping through a chink in the wall, beckoning to some good man for help, that an Immortal soul might be awakened (Dickens, I. 73).

The shining factories of Lowell, Massachusetts, perhaps again through Dickens's offices, became a necessary contrast to Manchester, physical and spiritual:

> Firstly there is a joint-stock piano in a great many of the boarding-houses. Secondly, nearly all these young ladies subscribe to circulating libraries. Thirdly, they have got up among themselves a periodical called The Lowell Offering, 'A repository of original articles, written exclusively by females actively employed in the mills,' – which is duly printed, published, and sold; and whereof I brought away from Lowell four hundred good solid pages, which I have read from beginning to end (Dickens, I. 159–60).

Other shining comparisons to British institutions were the asylums for the insane in Boston and Philadelphia, the Philadelphia penitentiary, the New York and Massachusetts state school systems. Utopia met with mixed reactions, though, as it was seen in the form of Girard College near Philadelphia, founded with enough ideals to bring it up to the high level Boston had set for the travellers, but somewhat too pretentious in the final analysis. Most visitors only cited its articles of incorporation, which forbade in perpetuity any influence upon its orphan scholars by ministers of any established religion, but some found the fancy polished marble architecture emblematic of the college's pretension in general.

> They contrived to overstep the terms of the will, and in building a marble palace, have so crippled their resources, that the chief purpose of the testator has been well nigh frustrated (Alexander Mackay, 93).

Marianne Finch couldn't help noticing that although the edifice was designed to last for ever like most American public buildings – and she regrets the thought even as it comes to her – it would make a magnificent ruin (257).

Washington offered a similar architectural allegory, calling forth the same response that Brasilia has brought forth in the decade just past.

> Take the worst parts of the City Road and Pentonville, preserving all their oddities, but especially the small shops and dwellings, occupied there (but not in Washington) by furniture-brokers, keepers of poor eating-houses, and fanciers of birds. Burn the whole down; build it up again in wood and plaster; widen it a little; throw in part of St. John's Wood; put green

blinds outside all the private houses, with a red curtain and a white one in every window; plough up all the road; plant a great deal of coarse turf in every place where it ought *not* to be; erect three handsome buildings in stone and marble, anywhere, but the more entirely out of everybody's way the better; call one the Post Office, one the Patent Office and one the Treasury; make it scorching hot in the morning, and freezing cold in the afternoon, with an occasional tornado of wind and dust; leave a brick-field without the bricks, in all central places where a street may naturally be expected: and that's Washington . . . A . . . straggling row of houses . . . in a melancholy piece of waste ground and frowzy grass, which looks like a small piece of country that has taken to drinking and has quite lost itself . . . It is sometimes called the City of Magnificent Distances, but it might with greater propriety be termed the City of Magnificent Intentions (Dickens, I. 278–81). A country village which has gone mad, and flung itself in a kind of wild dishevelled way about the fields. A street does not *mean* a street, but simply a line of country where a street ought to be; . . . if you ask . . . and are directed to '21st Street,' you probably find your way, after interminable inquiries and wanderings, to a solitary dwelling upon a piece of waste land, and by degrees become aware of the fact that the house in question and 21st Street are synonymous . . . There are a few other public buildings dropped about . . . which stand white and staring, as if astonished at their own unnatural position: . . . it requires no ordinary effort of abstraction to recollect . . . that one is in the capital city of a great nation (Godley, 190–1).

Perhaps pretentious and raw, but appealingly open, none the less. The great majority of the visitors (eighteen out of twenty-three) called at the White House and were introduced to the President. All detail it with pride and even those who didn't call feel obliged to explain why they couldn't. They are met by none of the expected Life-Guards or security forces which causes some of them to take the occasion to multiply their own unimportance by such evident availability and conclude that the President ought not to bother, but they find no evidence that the President any more than Laura Bridgman or Emerson ever publicly regrets the time wasted.

They meet notable senators (chiefly Henry Clay and Daniel Webster) and look in on the halls of legislation just long enough to comment on the spittoons or the freedom of the nation's legislative system or both, depending upon their mood at the time.

Washington is for most of them travelling southward, a time of doubt. They are about to enter upon the slave states. The great theme of their travels is approaching. The first response to such a challenge is to lapse again into a physical allegory, seeing in the countryside of whatever slave state they pass into unmistakable ruin and decay in comparison with whatever free state they pass out of.

> The soil has been exhausted ... it is now little better than a sandy desert ... I was glad to the heart to find anything on which one of the curses of this horrible institution has fallen; and had greater pleasure in contemplating the withered ground, than the richest and most thriving cultivation in the same place could possibly have afforded me ... An air of ruin and decay abroad, which is inseparable from the system (Dickens, II. 15–16). The moment the stranger puts his foot in Virginia, he seems to have passed to an entirely new scene of action ... Is it prejudice, or preconceived opinion, that leads him to think that every thing around him wears a spiritless and even dilapidated aspect? Or is it that he sees aright ... the whole State seems to be afflicted with some ineradicable blight (Alexander Mackay, 250). Every-thing wore a dirty, slovenly appearance. Mangy ill-conditioned swine wander about the streets, seeking what they may devour, and heaps of filth were lying in the gutters (Everest, 87–8). Retarded development and apparent decay (Bishop, 127–8); an air of non-progressiveness, if not decay and desolation (C. Mackay, II. 37).

One traveller (Sturge, 95) notes 'the contrast' of passing from a free to a slave state even though he never ventures farther south than Washington. Even the rather neutral Sir Charles Lyell makes the observation by omission when he says that 'Virginia seems to be rousing herself' (206), and the Hon. Amelia M. Murray, a firm convert to slavery's virtues, can only manage to see improvement in 'tone of voice and choice of words and pronunciation ... much more like old England as one proceeds further South' (202). One abolitionist even connects American inquisitiveness, which virtually every traveller notes, to slavery:

> This inquisitiveness prevails more in the slave than in the free states, and originates, I believe, in the fidgetty anxiety they feel

about their slaves. The stranger must be well catechised, lest he should prove to be an Abolitionist come to give the slaves a sly lesson in geography (Davies, 167).

As such comments indicate, most of the travellers come with a fully-formed attitude towards slavery as surely as they come with luggage for the trip. Most believe in abolition and find in everything they see an argument to support their position; some suspend revelation of this attitude so that it may coincide with their visit to a slave auction; none retain perfect neutrality. It is like the mixed belief and doubt with which they greet the New England Utopias: Dickens came with the determined intention to confirm his belief in Utopian industry and charitable institutions, the cancer of slavery and the god of Mammon – he finds just what he expected and wanted, and can debunk America's constitutional superiority to England (the words of the Constitution fail to be borne out by the deeds of the legislature) and at the same time retain his right to praise the potential Utopia in isolated institutions. It is as if the arguments have been memorized before leaving England and only the object-lessons remain to be inserted. Slavery can be even worse and Lowell can be even better, but a change in argument is more or less forestalled. Miss Murray tells her readers that she is neutral at the outset, but the terms of her statement do not lend her much credence:

> I know you will not think me upholding Slavery; Christianity will and must subdue it – not by teaching us to vilify and persecute those less fortunate of our brethren who have had the curse of human possessions entailed upon them – but by enlightening the darkened, and instructing the ignorant; and even (if that should be necessary) making such property valueless in a commercial point of view ... And I firmly believe there are few, very few, even in the South, who will not hail with joy the moment of emancipation – a movement at present delayed by doubts and fears. This is my first view of a vexed question; I may alter it – I may change it altogether; but in the meanwhile, such as it is, I give it (39).

Had this been true, her journey would have been a Road to Damascus, but she has neither conversion nor revelation. She doesn't like the black's 'monkey face' from the start:

The Creator of men formed them for labour under guidance (221); They are tricky, idle, and dirty (209); 'The pig will never grow into the lion' (210); I very much doubt if freedom will ever make the black population, in the mass, anything more than a set of grown-up children (195).

Every black she talks to is rather magically transformed by her rendering into Stepanfetchit or Butterfly McQueen. She has, on the other hand, a firm and steady belief in the sanctity of the private property represented in human chattel:

We should bestow our compassion on the masters instead of on the slaves . . . [They] by no means enjoy the incubus with which circumstances have loaded them, and would be only too happy if they could supersede this black labour with white (195).

Such argument – either for abolition or for the 'institution' – can be without any evidence: some travellers never pass below Washington, but enter their arguments just the same. Remarkably few visit a plantation, considering the dominance of their great theme and the contemporary chic of Mrs Stowe; all too many find their strongest evidence in what they can see in the railway car and through its windows – prejudicial seating and shabby dwelling.

Predetermined positions lead to a rather rote-like journalism in most cases. Many of these give the reader the impression that either the travellers have edited their notes and jottings too heavily, so that their observations have been rendered 'suitable' to a central argument, or that the travellers spent little of their time really *seeing* anything other than what their unwritten Cook's Tour or their basic ideological positions required them to see.

The major exception – the point at which almost every journal takes on vitality – is in witnessing a slave auction. There is quite often the quality of epiphany to these portions of the accounts. They had read and they knew, but they had not believed until now that they could see the sale of one set of people by another set of people under absolutely everyday and ordinary circumstances, as if it were no more out of the ordinary than the sale of beef cattle. Here the reality goes so far beyond the expectations, the 'institution' becomes so tangibly present, that the visitors are driven into dramatic rendering – the device which gives Olmsted's *Our Slave States* so much of its power, but which most of the journalists generally avoid. Even the purplest prose and most mawkish appeal for sentiment can do little to damage the impact of these observations on the reader.

There must have been from 70 to 100, all young people, varying from 15 to 30 years of age. All (both men and women) were well dressed, to set them off to the best advantage ... The whole were arranged under a kind of verandah, having a foot-bench (about six inches high) to stand upon, and their backs resting against the wall. None were in any way tied or chained; but two white men ('soul-drivers', I suppose) were sauntering about in front of them, each with a cigar in his mouth, a whip under his arm, and his hands in his pockets, looking out for purchasers. ... It was between twelve and one in the day; but there was no crowd, not even a single boy or girl looking on, – so common and every-day was the character of the scene. As we moved along in front of this sable row, one of the white attendants (though my wife had hold of my arm) said to me, with all the *nonchalance* of a Smithfield cattle-drover, 'Looking out for a few niggers this morning?' Never did I feel my manhood so insulted ... But I endeavoured to affect indifference, and answered in a don't-care sort of tone, 'No, I am not particularly in want of any to-da —.' I could scarcely finish the sentence ... The next 'lot' was a family, consisting of the husband, a man slightly coloured, about 30 years of age, the wife about 25, quite black, and reminding me forcibly of an excellent woman in my own congregation, and a little girl about 4 years of age, and a child in the arms. They were told to mount the platform. As they obeyed, I was attracted by a little incident, which had well nigh caused my feelings to betray me ... Parents of England, let me tell it you, and enlist your sympathies on behalf of oppressed and outraged humanity. It was that of a father helping up, by the hand, *his own little girl to be exposed for sale!* 'Now, who bids for this family? Title good – guaranteed free from the vices and maladies provided against by law. The man is an excellent shoemaker – can turn his hand to anything, – and his wife is a very good house-servant. Who bids for the lot? 500 dollars bid for them – 600 dollars – only 600 dollars – 700 dollars offered for them.' But the price ultimately mounted up to 1,125 dollars. – 'Going for 1,125 dollars – once – twice – gone for 1,125 dollars' (Davies, 23–4, 51–2).

It is the power that the visitors perhaps didn't know they had, that one moment of rendered experience is worth a hundred atrocity stories picked up in the railway. Only Dickens and Trollope and some few of the others (Marianne Finch and Davies, in particular) exploit the potential of the dramatic and descriptive, giving their arguments the kind of power that no number of second-hand tales could attain.

Only by ignoring such particulars, could the pro-slavery visitors pursue their argument at all: Miss Murray doesn't go to an auction, neither does Henry Ashworth, the touring manufacturer who eventually delivers his experiences as a course of lectures before the members of the Bolton Mechanics' Institution. He works on the 'big picture', the economic and geographical justification for slavery, but at the cost of any enlivening particular details. The Abolitionists are 'receivers of stolen goods' (45) and the slaves become a happy function of economic necessity, an essential cog in the international machine:

> Upon these plantations, 600,000 negro slaves have made the people of all nations become tributaries to their power, and almost wholly reliant upon their annual success in the growth of a cotton crop. Upon this handful of coloured people, our manufacturers mainly depend for a vegetable product which employs the hands, fills the mouths, and clothes the bodies of millions of the human race, who might otherwise go half naked, or half fed (85).

Presumably the slaves were to be happy in the thought that their labour provided the greatest good for the greatest number. The geographical rightness of slavery was a similarly grand argument: only black labour was suitable to the climate; they were not fit for freedom and if they were freed, they would not provide the labour. Even the poor planters were not equipped to remain in the swamps of the agricultural goldmine and had to go to Saratoga or otherwise north for six months out of the year, 'residing amongst the mixed company of the various hotels, involving a fearful inroad upon their domestic habits' (94–5). He shares Miss Murray's feeling that Britain should save its pity for the owners, not the slaves.

The general tenor of British abolitionists is basically gradualist, less radical than their American counterparts. Emancipation was a goal, but immediate universal manumission without preparing the slaves by education or training, it was thought, would produce hardship on the blacks thus freed and financial disaster for the owners. They would receive no recompense for their property and would be unable to convert their livelihood to a free-labour economy. Gradual emancipation was the practical aim usually advocated (see p. 130) and immediate legislative reform, they felt, was necessary only for the law and the practice which disturbed them most: that slaves could not, under penalty of law, be taught to read or write, and that the social fabric of the black family, such as it was, was destroyed by separate sales of members of families. To contest the latter, most pro-slavery visitors simply held it was not true, and cited for evidence conversations with slave-owners and auctioneers (BSB reports one such conversation with an auctioneer in New Orleans, p. 70). As for the law, pro-slavery visitors either ignored it, cited the 'play-schools' formed by the masters' children on plantations ('The little "niggers", ... could any day be seen running to and from school, carrying their books in straps', Ashworth, 45) or asserted that the law was not observed:

> To this remark one of our friends replied, that there was upon the statute book a law to that effect, – not a recent enactment, but an unrepealed statute enacted by the British when the country was a colony; but that in effect this law was now no law at all, as its provisions had long since ceased to be regarded (44).

Such laws had, in reality, been enacted as a response to the fear of slave uprising following Nat Turner's rebellion; that they were enforced seems evident from the lack of any schooling of slaves, but only one prosecution is noted in travel-journals: that of a Mrs Douglas of Norfolk, Virginia, said by one of the American abolitionists to have been confined in a penitentiary for teaching free blacks to read (Redpath, 184).

What joined abolitionist and pro-slavery visitors was their sense that slavery was not a phenomenon of these two decades. Almost all of them referred to its roots in the eighteenth century and not a few of them suggested that England's earlier domination of the colonies had been responsible for the continuation of slavery.

> Under every aspect the presence of the coloured race in the same country with the whites is a bitter curse to it: and we must not forget that Virginia owes this to our government; for bill after bill, prohibiting the slave-trade, was passed by the Virginian legislature, and negatived by the crown; so that we have no right to taunt her with the effects of the slave-trade, except so far as the continued existence of them contradicts her ultra-democratic theories, or so far as the evil which attends them is practically remediable (Godley, 213–14). England was then the mother-country, and, carrying on the slave-trade, required a market for her cargoes of slaves, and commanded the young American colonies to become this market (Bremer, 290). England bequeathed this system to her colonies, though she has nobly blotted it out from those which still own her sway; . . . it is encouraged by the cotton lords of Preston and Manchester (Bishop, 131). The enormously increasing demand for cotton in England caused a proportionate rise in the value of slave labour and of slaves . . . These simple facts fully dispose of the vaunted benevolence of those, who boast of their country having made the slave trade with Africa piracy – because they do silently and more cheaply at home what they had no further inducement to do with profit abroad (Grattan, 412).

Historical reasoning was then set to one side because, as with the hope for Utopia and the expectation of uncouth savages, the travellers held side by side – saw by binocular vision – their fault and American guilt: they had done something about theirs; America could surely clean its own house.

Binocular vision was the only sensible choice, and it gives these journals much of their life. The problem was how to see and render what was so similar to England and yet so different – the same language but the experience of some exotic Bohemia: how to admire and correct, know and see, judge and sympathize, believe and doubt. How to bring their cherished preconceived arguments and positions into line with the sights, facts and tales they encountered in travel, retain their historical superiority without relinquishing their idealistic enthusiasm for new ventures.

A point at which this binocular vision is most sharply tested (and generally doesn't work) is life on the Mississippi.

The return north (or in many cases, the trip south) follows Huck Finn's route in more senses than one. On the river the visitors find the beauties of virgin land, the hint of a savage countryside, an avenue which they broadly believe represents the division between civilization and savagery. But the journey is by steamboat and for most of the travellers this vessel becomes a Bunyanesque showboat of kinds and conditions of Americans. Each time they touch shore they see something there of what they imagine to be the frontier, the backwoods, Natty Bumppos and riverboat gamblers behind every waiting cotton bale, just out of earshot a vendetta consummated or a duel in progress. With such strange sights for their eyes, their affection for fact, generally vivid when it comes to slavery, retires completely in favour of their desire for excitement and, again, the hope for outrage and barbarism which was part of the original drive which had led them to these shores. Gullibility reaches its apex on the river.

As with the 'ruin and decay' they observed in crossing the Mason-Dixon Line, so with the moral corruption of the people. Because the river, the riverboats and their denizens are so new to them, they immediately draw the contrast between this and Boston and Philadelphia. Bishop Whipple, an American travelling the same route, sets the framework for this regional mythos.

> The people of the southern states are generally much more hospitable than northerners, and this difference must be attributed mainly to the fact that they are not such a money loving people. You do not see that low mean cupidity, that base selfishness so striking a characteristic of one portion of our restless Yankee brethren. But the energies of the south are crippled by the incubus of slavery (Whipple, 30).

Geographical remoteness is made to equal historical remoteness, and a Golden Age principle comes into play. Some, even some mild abolitionists, arrive at the idea of a feudal or chivalric frontier.

> [The Southerner] appears to desire to keep about him the days of chivalry of old (Whipple, 33). He is more chivalrous, that is to say, he has more of the old English feeling common in the days of the feudal system & crusades . . . He is generous to a

fault with his property, is fond of gaiety and pleasure & generally dislikes the routine of business. His habits are those of genteel idleness or of the man of leisure (43). It may be, too, that they have a little of the old Norman blood in them, which makes them such a fillibustering set; for the old States of the South were all aristocratically settled ... The black serfs were exactly according to their notions, and the class has still the same contempt for industry and trade that ever it had ... The Chivalry it is that is warlike, and fond of glory, striving to increase the government, naval, and military establishments, that its idle children may (as one of their own papers tells them) be able to exchange the small despotism of home, for that of the quarter-deck and the parade ground; gentlemen of high descent are they, and not the industrious farmers and artizans of the North, who work with their own hands. If there is anything that makes the republic work badly, and may hereafter produce mischief, it is this system of slavery. The evil has been ... that that one mediaeval institution has not been extirpated, incompatible as it is with the rest ... The accomplished gentleman, duellist, and gambler ... is just the stuff for a conspirator (Everest, 146–7).

Everest seems to insist on the chivalric and medieval elements so that he can bring his idea of the South into line with his theories on class – he can't bring himself to believe that class distinctions don't exist here as they do in England. His latter reference to gentleman, duellist and gambler, though, is connected to a strong strain of the myth of the river.

The people of Richmond are a peculiar people. They are proud and sensitive to a degree ... Their code of honour is so exceedingly strict that it requires the greatest circumspection to escape its violation. An offence which elsewhere would be regarded as of homeopathic proportions, is very apt to assume in Richmond the gravity of colossal dimensions; even a coolness between parties is dangerous, as having a fatal tendency speedily to ripen into a deadly feud. Once arrived at this point, a personal encounter is inevitable, unless, to avoid it, one party or the other is induced to quit the city. It is curious enough to witness the cool and matter-of-course way in which even the ladies will speculate upon the necessities for, and the probabilities of, a hostile meeting between such and such parties, and in which, when they hear of a duel, they will tell you that they long foresaw it, and that it could not be avoided. After all, this state of things, although it may indicate less of a healthy habit than of a morbid sensibility, gives to Richmond society a chivalrous and romantic cast, which is rarely to be met with in matter-of-fact America (A. Mackay, 254).

The last line contains the clue: tales of duelling, devil-may-care honour, the Rhett Butler streak in Southern manhood, provide exciting relief from what BSB complains about as the 'everlasting shore' of the river journey. Feuds (even as Huck Finn found) are one result of this code:

I heard that people were often shot, and no notice taken of it. Feuds existed between families; and one was mentioned, in consequence of which twelve persons had, at different times, lost their lives (Everest, 91).

Duels are another; again Whipple establishes the mythic outline for the British.

A few miles from St. Marys we passed Cumberland Beach, so renowned as the theatre of many bloody duels. It was here that Palosti and Babcok fought [a drunken quarrel which had really taken place on Amelia Island and involved a Dr. Pelot]. Cruel horrid custom thus to butcher & destroy men for the false code of honour. Honour! It is a vague idea the duellist has of honour. He does not know whether its location be in his head or heels (Whipple, 29). Another instance ... two men had a slight difficulty about some hogs. They became enraged & meeting each other both fired at the same time. The one was killed & the other dangerously wounded (30). There have been several duels ... the last between two boys at the Naval school [Annapolis], who fired six shots each, and did not desist till one of them was shot through the neck: he is still in a precarious state (Godley, 191). Shortly before my arrival at Louisville, a young man, son of one of the wealthiest proprietors in the neighbourhood, went to the school, where his brother, who was a scholar, had been punished, and shot the master dead with a revolver (Everest, 91).

Lynchings complete the roster of lawless anecdote:

'In these out-of-the-way places, people cannot afford to lose much time; when a man has a troublesome negro, he calls his neighbours together, and they just bring him under a strong branch of the black-jack tree, which is very elastic, tie one end of the rope to it, and put a noose at the other end under his ear then let loose, and up he goes.' I gave a nervous sign of horror, and the man next me laughed, and added, 'It is so easily done, you would think nothing of it if you saw it. I have seen seven swinging from one tree' (Everest, 103).

The counterpart to the north-south division of industry (or avarice) and chivalry (or cruelty) is a division between rule of law and outlawry.

I heard nothing of these fighting and murdering propensities while I was in the North, and have reason to think they are confined within the limits of the slave States (Everest, 106). The impress of the strict morals of the Puritan founders of the New England commonwealths on the manners of their descendants, is still very marked. Swearing is seldom heard, and duelling has been successfully discountenanced, although they are in constant communication with the southern states, where both these practices are common, though much less so than formerly (Lyell, I. 127).

It should not be assumed that all of these were tall tales: BSB relates some that seem to be whoppers (see p. 57–8, 7 December) but which can be traced back to an essential root of truth. But the mythic element is strong. The story of the Vicksburg lynchings is picked up by half a dozen journals. The point is the relish with which the traveller picks up such stories and proceeds to generalize from them – not just to national mores and principles, but to the individuals on his boat.

It is the slave States that grow their crops of bowie knife and revolver men, fillibusters, and so forth (Everest, 106). Such a company as I find on board this boat if assembled together in England under similar circumstances, with the incessant drinking of beer & spirits which would be resorted to for companionship & pastime, would be attended with boisterous rudeness, & inevitable collisions. – The superior education in America will be thought by some, & the concealed bowie knife & revolver will be said by others, to account for the courtesy & forbearance of my fellow passengers, but I think the absence of stimulants to be the one great perserver of the peace (Cobden, 158). One hears of bowie-knives and revolvers continually, and I was assured that nine-tenths of the party carried them in their pockets. How far this ratio was the correct one, I had no means of ascertaining, but a man with whom I happened to be conversing, after fumbling in his pocket, as I thought, for his pocket-handkerchief, pulled out a revolver to fire at a duck that was sitting on the water; so it is probable that the custom is not uncommon (Everest, 91).

Cobden's comments on the function of liquor and concealed weapons in law and order was but one explanation. Others, of course, connected it to the chivalrous code and to the destructive disregard for human life instilled in the society by slavery. Dickens's explanation, though more vague, had more of the ring of truth – both factual and mythical.

The following dialogue I have held a hundred times: 'Is it not a very disgraceful circumstance that such a man as So and So should be acquiring a large property by the most infamous and odious means, and notwithstanding all the crimes of which he has been guilty, should be tolerated and abetted by your Citizens? he is a public nuisance, is he not?' 'Yes, sir.' 'A convicted liar?' 'Yes sir.' 'He has been kicked, and cuffed, and caned?' 'Yes sir.' 'And he is utterly dishonourable, debased, and profligate?' 'Yes sir.' 'In the name of wonder, then, what is his merit?' 'Well, sir, he is a smart man.' In like manner, all kinds of deficient and impolitic usages, are referred to the national love of trade; though, oddly enough, it would be a weighty charge against a foreigner that he regarded the Americans as a trading people (Dickens, II. 292–3).

The scoundrels, the 'fillibusters' or freebooters, the renegades, were all traceable back to the great God Mammon of Dickens's induction, the 'almighty dollar' which runs as a leit-motif through a number of the visitors' generalizations. The frontier especially, with its lure of big profit and the lawlessness of distance from authority, seemed to attract the scoundrel fringe: 'one half of the population of most modern towns in Florida are ruined spendthrifts and too many of the balance are rogues and scoundrels' (Whipple, 42). According to this line of mythical reasoning there was something of a vicious circle: the dollar moved the smart dealers to the frontier (or the river), the smart dealers made the society there, the society elected the smart dealers as its legislature and the legislature made further laws to promote smart dealing.

Dickens takes the word of the newspapers for the lawlessness of the legislative assembly:

> Member of the Council for Brown county was shot dead *on the floor* of the Council chamber, by ... Member from Grant county. *The affair* grew out of a nomination for Sheriff of Grant county ... Mr. Arndt then made a blow at Vinyard, who stepped back a pace, drew a pistol, and shot him dead ... Meetings have been held in different counties of Wisconsin, denouncing the *practice of secretly bearing arms in the legislative chambers of the country* (Dickens, II. 268–9).

Davies, since he sees the Louisiana legislature first-hand, is more convincing.

> [Nowhere,] in the Old World or in the New, did I see an assemblage of worse-looking men. They seemed fitted for any deeds of robbery, blood, and death. Several distinguished duellists were pointed out to me; among them Colonel Crane, an old man, who had repeatedly fought with Mr. Bowie, the inventer of the 'Bowie knife', and had killed several men in personal combat! The motion before the house just at that time was for the release from prison of a Mr. Simms, who a few days before had violently assaulted one of the members in the lobby. He was released accordingly. Who will not pity the 200,000 slaves of this State, who are at the 'tender mercies' of these sanguinary men? (Davies, 76).

The only measure of lawlessness which exceeded lay beyond the river, and this was *terra incognita* to most of the British travellers. They had heard tell of the West and when they were on the river or in outlying districts such as Florida or Mississippi, wanted what they saw to be *almost* as lawless, the local scoundrel to be *almost* as romantic and reckless:

> Such scenes may be worthy of Texas, but an American must blush at such scenes in this land of light & freedom (Whipple, 30). Nowhere this side of Texas can you find so many rascals who live by their wits (42). It is seldom, indeed, that they imitate, in their personal warfare, the savage brutalities of the south-western States; their quarrels, generally speaking, taking some time to mature, and the parties, when the day of reckoning at length comes, fighting like gentlemen, instead of like tigers or hyenas (A. Mackay, 254–5).

For the British traveller the river anticipates the Wild West in a need for American lawlessness as surely as it serves as its surrogate in *Huckleberry Finn*. The scoundrels and 'revolver men' are there: the Indians are missing because the visitors seem unable to envision them in any terms other than the Eastern Seaboard's myth of the Vanishing American.

In a low ground among the hills, is a valley known as 'Bloody Run', from a terrible conflict with the Indians which once occurred there. It is a good place for such a struggle, and, like every other spot I saw, associated with any legend of that wild people now so rapidly fading from the earth, interested me very much (Dickens, II. 18–19). They loved as did our fathers the scenes of childhood & the graves of their fathers. When will the cupidity & cruelty of white men cease. Never, no never till the last lone Indian has gone to the spirit land (Whipple, 21). I know of no subject strictly national in the United States which seems to possess so little interest at present as the situation, political, social, and moral, of the aboriginal inhabitants of the country. The Indian tribes are gradually fading from the earth, dissolving like shadows in a distant obscurity. They have nothing inherent in their character to gain for them an abiding place in the feelings of mankind. They have altogether failed to bear out the fantastic imaginings of poets and romance writers. Had they really possessed the attributes ascribed to them, they would have taken a permanent stand in the admiration and affection of the world. But a couple of centuries have made it evident that they are truly an inferior race of beings, incapable of anything great, unable to work out a destiny or stamp a character beyond that of a sluggish and dogged originality, deficient in dignity, and unfit to blend with the plastic elements of civilization (Grattan, II. 231).

History was to give the Indians a chance to make Grattan's words seem empty, but for him and the other visitors at the moment, the redskins ('They were really red, that is to say, they were *painted*; but when washed, the red man is by no means red, but light brown', Mrs Pulszky helpfully notes, I. 18–21) were at the moment not much more than Chingachgooks left over. The best point on the unofficial Cook's Tour to take them in is Washington, as they visit the President.

The chiefs and braves of four different tribes were here, and two of them had brought their squaws along with them; clad in their skins and blankets, or ornamented with feather crowns, with their clubs and pipes, crouching on the floor, they offered a most picturesque scene ... After all, the Indians seemed pretty well comforted by receiving silver medals, and a large star-spangled flag. As the squaws were unexpected visitors, Mrs. Fillmore had nothing to give them but sugar-plums (Pulszky, I. 18–23).

Marianne Finch locates a few on something more like home ground, near Saratoga, New York, and she displays the kind of interest in them one might expect of a spectator at a raree-show near Charing Cross in the eighteenth century.

The men were making bows and arrows, which was quite *comme il faut*; but to see the old squaws sewing in spectacles, and the young ones handling needles and scissors, as daintily as boarding-school misses, seemed quite an innovation on the proprieties of Indian life, and has doubtless been duly anathematized by the 'friends of order' belonging to the race. I made several attempts at conversation with these gentle dames, but always found their knowledge of English was confined to the subject of currency. They told me exactly how many cents made a dollar; and on my taking up a watchpocket that one of them finished while I was there, she showed me which of the pieces of silver in my purse would pay for it (Finch, 116–17).

Indians were a sight which the visitors seemed to feel that their readers would expect them to seek out – like the Shakers – and they do so rather dutifully. They aren't, after all, of the moment, any more than the Shakers, and when they find them, they are a little sad and inevitably disappointing. The Shakers don't dance orgiastically, but only shuffle rhythmically; the Indians aren't really red and they wear spectacles.

Beyond the itinerary there are generalizations to be drawn and more sweeping judgments to be made on manners and morals. Most visitors find the newspapers amazing. Dickens uses them to the hilt, quoting page after page of advertisements for runaway slaves and random reports of violence, but then turns around and denounces the press for keeping down the level of public enlightenment.

But while that Press has its evil eye in every house, and its black hand in every appointment in the state, from a president to a postman; while, with ribald slander for its only stock in trade, it is the standard literature of an enormous class, who must find their reading in a newspaper, or they will not read at all; so long must its odium be upon the country's head, and so long must the evil it works, be plainly visible in the Republic (Dickens, II. 296).

Others find that there are just too many newspapers or that they seem to know too much – more than the government.

Literature in general is subject to a similar mixed response. Outside Boston, Dickens concludes that, although the people seem to be 'very proud of their poets', they are at heart a 'trading people' and it doesn't really matter – they don't read them. Trollope complains of the opposite difficulty: literature is foisted upon him in trains.

A young man enters during the journey, – for the trade is carried out while the cars are travelling, as is also a very brisk trade in lollipops, sugar-candy, apples, and ham sandwiches, – the young tradesman enters the car firstly with a pile of magazines or of novels bound like magazines. These are chiefly the 'Atlantic', published at Boston, 'Harper's Magazine', published at New York, and a cheap series of novels published at Philadelphia. As he walks along he flings one at every passenger. An Englishman, when he is first introduced to this manner of trade, becomes much astonished. He is probably reading, and on a sudden he finds a fat, fluffy magazine, very unattractive in its exterior, dropped on to the page he is perusing. I thought at first that it was a present from some crazed philanthropist, who was thus endeavouring to disseminate literature. But I was soon undeceived. The bookseller, having gone down the whole car and the next, returned, and beginning again where he had begun before, picked up either his magazine or else the price of it. Then, in some half-hour, he came again, with an armful or basket of books, and distributed them in the same way. They were generally novels, but not always. I do not think that any endeavour is made to assimilate the book to the expected customer. The object is to bring the book and the man together, and in this way a very large sale is effected (Trollope, 270).

Trains in general are found inferior to English railways – cold, uncomfortable, jolting and noisy – and those who fail to admire the elegance of the floating hotels of the Mississippi, the steamboats, have similar complaints about them, and about their too many meals and too much food. Hotels are apparently almost on a par with English accommodations because they come in for little adverse criticism.

But the American phenomenon most noticed (other than slavery) – and here again there is Dickens to thank, the trail-blazer of the Cook's Tour – is expectoration.

As Washington may be called the head-quarters of tobacco-tinctured saliva, the time is come when I must confess, without any disguise, that the prevalence of those two odious practices of chewing and expectorating began about this time to be anything but agreeable, and soon became most offensive and sickening . . . In the courts of law, the judge has his spittoon, the crier his, the witness his, and the prisoner his; while the jurymen and spectators are provided for, as so many men who in the course of nature must desire to spit incessantly. In the hospitals, the students of medicine are requested, by notices upon the wall, to eject their tobacco juice into the boxes provided for that purpose, and not to discolour the stairs . . . On board this steamboat, there were two young gentlemen . . . who planted two seats in the middle of the deck, at a distance of some four paces apart; took out their tobacco-boxes; and sat down opposite each other, to chew. In less than a quarter of an hour's time, these hopeful youths had shed about them on the clean boards, a copious shower of yellow rain; clearing, by that means, a kind of magic circle, within whose limits no intruders dared to come, and which they never failed to refresh and re-refresh before a spot was dry. This being before breakfast, rather disposed me, I confess, to nausea (Dickens, I. 272–4). The floor is regularly incrusted with its daily succession of abominable deposits; so much so, that one might almost smoke a pipe from its scrapings . . . I was once on my way from Baltimore to Washington, when two men got in at the half-way station, somewhat the worse for liquor, and the first thing that one of them did on seating himself, was to take out his quid, and trace his initials with it upon the window, surrounding them afterwards with a framework of flourishes; conduct which seemed to excite but little disgust, many near him laughing, but only regarding it as one of the stupid things that men 'a little sprung' would sometimes do (A. Mackay, 101). Their dirty habit of squirting tobacco juice around them and other *peculiarities*, to which the *ladies* of the other hemisphere are unaccustomed (Cunynghame, 44). That filthy, and disgusting characteristic by which Americans are so well known . . . is still sufficiently prominent, to justify an American philosopher, in defining man to be a spitting animal, rather than a 'cooking animal', or a 'laughing animal' (Finch, 297).

The observation becomes so customary that eventually it is honoured by omission: 'There was neither smoking nor spitting', observes Everest, to underline the civilized quality of the train to Boston.

The tobacco theme assures the reader of these journals once again that the majority of the English came to see what they expected, to observe what they knew and to verify with their own eyes, rather than to discover, feel or know anew. Some came on business, to investigate their investment in the Illinois Central Railroad (Cobden), to look into cheap land (Barclay), to check on the organization of American abolitionists (Sturge), in deputation from the Free Church of Scotland (Lewis). Some were (Bremer and Murray), it was suspected, investigating the States for Queen Victoria. Those who were experienced writers, made the best record of their travels because they knew how monotonous the journal as a genre could be and enlivened it with a fresh eye and bracing prose (Dickens) or a consistency of mind and a blend of rendering and argument (Trollope). There are a few surprises: the Hon. Amelia M. Murray writes a journal filled with fake Road-to-Damascus conversions to the slaveowners' cause; her journal is difficult to like because of her smugness, her inaccuracy, her U-attitudes – all the complaints that Madame Bodichon registers against her at the time (p. 99). But in spite of this, her account lives in the memory because of the detailed quality of her observations, the precision of her eye (in spite of her tin ear for dialect) and the image of the proper lady trudging off into the wilds in pursuit of yet another fossil or another dainty for the greenhouse. Marianne Finch, too (she of the *comme il faut* Indians), wins through by charm, eye and character.

Barbara Smith Bodichon came on a wedding trip, but (never one to waste a trip on one purpose alone) had other aims as well: she wished to return with her preconceptions sharpened, to back up the opinions she already held with out-of-the-way observations of detail. She had been George Eliot's model for the physical outlines of the heroine of *Romola*, but similarity quickly becomes a set of distinctions. She is similar only in vague outlines of spirit. Romola's frustrations are those of a woman imprisoned by the fact of being a woman in a male world; but that Barbara was a woman was a source of her freedom and a key to her action. Frustration and entrapment for her came from elsewhere: the imprisonment of the Cause, the celebrity of activism. Zeal could never appear to be less than intense, public dedication always had to be the same – even when she was tired or bored or sick. In America she met the activist and intellectual aristocracy and talked, talked, talked in salons, at dinner parties, at evening gatherings for the Cause – the sometimes confused combination of Abolition, Women's Rights and Unitarianism. The intellectual festival which brought her travels to a close in Philadelphia, Boston and New York must have been a bit stifling in the uniform agreement she met on all sides.

But she escaped this containment in the South: in the adversity of opinion, the stupidity of planters' wives, the helplessness of freed slaves. It is these early portions of the journal which give it its peculiar value. The Bodichons came to America as did the other British visitors, fully instructed by travel books and travellers' accounts, seeking to see the future with their own eyes, but already dubious of some of the books' bland certainty that all was well, that reports of cruelty were exaggerated, that the slave states were working out their destinies patiently and humanely. Barbara was not predisposed to see only the dark side, but neither was she satisfied with easy answers. The letters which form the journal had several purposes – news to relatives, raw material for articles – but first of all, the impetus which is behind the best journals: the desire to organize and intensify experience by writing it down, the construction of an attitude toward a body of experience in the act of forming it into a narrative. She wanted a record for herself, fuel for the persuasion of others and a narrative for history. Reports which came to her were occasionally exaggerated or false, but she would not exaggerate what she saw herself or traffic in distortions, no matter how useful such distortion might be as ammunition for the cause. Hearsay provided information on plantation slavery and general national and regional characteristics, and for these the historian would do better to turn again to Olmsted. But her own rambles led her into much more difficult marginal areas: negro churches, immigrant workers, small schools, freed slaves. In her observation of these, there is much that is original and her honesty is not to be questioned. And there is a loving arguer's clarity of mind and a painter's sharp visual observation.

There is a nineteenth-century fashion which affects our judgment of all of the journals: those that were less 'prepared' for publication, those that were given less chance to have their observation subordinated to their message, come through more clearly than the 'written' journals and the canned opinions. Barbara Bodichon, in the rewritten passages of her journal which she published in the *Englishwoman's Journal* succumbed to the temptation to re-cast moment into evidence. Had she managed to rush the journal into print as she wanted to do, it is likely that much of its life would have been suppressed in the process.

But she didn't. She stands up rather well in this now-distinguished, now-ill-assorted company. She meets the people – the slave on the block, the mulatto family down the street, the old lady in the black church and the crazy Mrs Sillery – runs into Colonel Haskell and records his advances, characterizes her fellow-passengers just enough so that their words take on a bit more drama than most journalists, even Olmsted, generally manage. And the Americans she seeks out to meet are, in cross-section, remarkable. There's no Cook's Tour to guide her here – and she goes beyond the required visits to Lucretia Mott and Emerson to a list of distinction: about seventy-five per cent of the men and women she meets are listed in the *Dictionary of American Biography*. The Unitarian-Transcendentalist-Abolitionist-Women's Rights Axis was remarkably broad as she observed it, and it moved her into close connection with the company of the forces that were moving the nation.

The woman who emerges is not really very likeable – most of us would like to talk to her and would probably be very taken with listening to her, but we might find it hard to see her as a friend. Her journal is another matter. She sees, perhaps better than any of her fellow citizens except Dickens, the United States at the time of a critical pause, and the prickly personality (which I am the first to admit, sometimes is difficult) is not so much a barrier to that clear view as it is the medium through which its truth and value emerge.

And beyond the importance her intellectual activism and her concrete contributions lend to her opinions, the excitement of her personality and her mind emerge from this account as an independent demand upon our attention. She is simply a woman who matters, who is determined to matter in as many ways and in as many places as her considerable energies and talents and her limited time will permit.

CHAPTER 2

BARBARA LEIGH SMITH
BODICHON
1827–91

Barbara Leigh Smith married Eugène Bodichon, M.D., in July of 1857 and a few weeks later set out on a wedding trip (*cum* painting, fact-finding, view-hunting and ideal-sharing) through North America.

> I am one of the cracked people of the world [she had told her aunt], and I like to herd with the cracked . . . queer Americans, democrats, socialists, artists, poor devils or angels; and am never happy in an English genteel family life. I try to do it like other people, but I long always to be off on some wild adventure, or long to lecture on a tub in St. Giles, or go to see the Mormons, or ride off into the interior on horseback alone and leave the world for a month. I want to see what sort of world this God's world is.

She had been attracted to Dr Bodichon as much for their common goals and shared principles as she had by love. He was a French colonial in Algiers of an old bourgeois Breton family, Bonapartist on his father's side, royalist and Catholic on his mother's. As a medical student in Paris he had travelled with republicans and had known Louis Blanc; then had been a corresponding member of the Chamber of Deputies for Algeria and had worked for the abolition of slavery in the colony. His election address, published in 1848, was perhaps even more idealistic than Barbara's credo quoted above, although a bit less abandoned: 'Mes espérances pour l'avenir – le genre humain ne formera plus qu'une seule famille.' Barbara had found within this consonant idealism a 'cracked' quality, too. 'He is a man who gathers flowers daily for his own pleasure; who walks twenty miles to hear the hyenas laugh.' He was dark and perhaps attractive in a formidable way, 'tall, grave, almost sombre in aspect, and very eccentric in dress . . . and has black hair as thick as a Newfoundland dog's coat. Some people think the docteur ugly and terrific.' One of these described him as a 'he-hag', another as a girl's childhood idea of Moses. But Barbara found him 'the handsomest man ever created', 'by temperament sensitive, irritable, passionate, violent and reserved', 'the reverse of me in all natural gifts'.

In all this there is a suggestion of menace which the doctor deliberately accentuated with an air of romantic mystery and exotic *panache* – wearing the burnous in Alabama or a blue peasant blouse at Scalands (Barbara's country cottage near

Robertsbridge), leading a group of desert sheiks into a London party, or, as reported by William Michael Rossetti, walking into the country 'without a hat and *with* a jackal enacting the part of a semi-domestic dog'. The same instinct for self-dramatization emerged in conversation:

> Dr. Bodichon of Algiers had a serious theory for improving the world in the shortest possible time, by the painless extinction of all useless human beings. He would have juries, including a large proportion of men of science, to decide on the fitness of this person or that to live . . . Madame Bodichon said to me in the midst of one of her husband's discourses on scientific homicide, – 'he wouldn't himself drown a kitten!'

Burnous, jackal and theory could all have been, in part, the response of a male who, because he sincerely believed in female equality, couldn't call attention to himself in the customary male chauvinist fashion. And in the presence of Barbara he needed a little attention called to himself. He was at first uncomfortable in England because of his poor English, and felt increasingly alien from Barbara's friends – even the most activist of them. He honoured their marital agreement – independence for both with apparently no obligation of either to adopt the other's interests – but as time went on, he suffered England and lived for the Algerian season, as Barbara suffered the time away from England (despite her love for the African scenery) and returned eager for the activist concerns of home.

Contemporary advice held that it was 'the privilege of a married woman to be able to show by the most delicate attentions, how much she feels her husband's superiority to herself not by mere personal services . . . but by a respectful deference to his opinion, a willingly imposed silence when he speaks.' (According to this position, Barbara clearly shouldn't even have mentioned that kitten.) Even 'a hightly gifted woman' ought not to 'exhibit the least disposition to presume upon such gifts', lest she rouse her husband's 'jealousy of her importance'. But Barbara, highly gifted, was also highly opinionated: marriage was a state, she had once held, by which a woman passed from freedom 'into the condition of a slave'. She softened this somewhat in making her settlement with the Doctor, but still drew a sharp line between her independence and the restriction of a conventional marriage. John Thomas instructed her in a letter to correct her name to include the Doctor's, and she replied in one of the letters that make up this journal:

> I believe he is wrong as a matter of law. I do not think there is any law to oblige a woman to bear the name of her husband at all, and probably none to prevent keeping the old name. To use it is very useful, for I have earned a right to Barbara Smith and am more widely known than I had any idea of . . . Dr. says he should think it folly for me to use his name except as a convenience in society, and if we have a line of English descendants they will be Bodichon-Smiths (22 March).

Such an arrangement seems peculiar for the 1850s until one knows the man, and, especially, the woman involved. But peculiar as it is, it came hard on the heels of a relationship even more unconventional, which called up for Barbara more critical questions of independence on the one hand and unconventional settlement (or rather, projected settlement) on the other. Barbara had been engaged in a liaison with John Chapman, a married man with children who continually augmented his marital arrangement with this affair and that, at home and away, with an ever-shifting cast of women, up to and including Marian Evans, soon to become George Eliot. The Chapman-Bodichon relationship is difficult to chart in terms of male dominance or female freedom because it is difficult enough to understand in simple erotic terms. Only Chapman's letters survive of their love-letters (surely one of the oddest erotic correspondences in history).[1] Since Barbara's replies have not come to light, one can barely glimpse what her letters were like through Chapman's responses, a dark glass through which it is most difficult to glimpse anything at all. Chapman is very nearly an egomaniac. He continually obscures Barbara's feelings by his own over-elaborate response to them. But the affair is worth some detailed attention for the light it casts on her later character and career.

John Chapman, who had been a medical student (perhaps in Paris) and had studied at St Bartholomew's, had taken over the editorship of the *Westminster Review* in 1851. His marriage to Susanna Brewitt in 1843 had not been happy, and he found relief from it in various philandering arrangements, some of them quite domestic in his home in Blandford Square, apparently with the full knowledge of his wife. He was juggling one such ménage rather successfully until he tried to keep too many oranges in the air at one time when Elisabeth Tilley, the resident mistress (and not Susanna) became jealous of his affections for Marian Evans, who had been taken on as assistant editor for the *Westminster*, moved in with the Chapmans for editorial convenience and then became something more than an assistant.

Chapman seems to have blamed this trouble on the close quarters rather than on the size of the cast, because when he established a liaison with Barbara Smith (perhaps as early as 1853) he made no effort to bring her into the household. The household had become somewhat simpler: Marian Evans was a thing of the past and was now firmly ensconced with George Henry Lewes (this became part of Chapman's ammunition with Barbara: 'We shall be happy yet. Lewes and M. E. seemed to be perfectly so'); Elisabeth was apparently still on the scene but not in the picture. But the brazen and battle-scarred adulterer still employed precautions worthy of a French farce. He insisted that Barbara's friend Anna Mary Howitt address some of her letters to him, that they had to meet in odd places on weekends, that secrecy be the rule.

On her side Barbara was being plagued by troubles and doubts, female troubles and doubts about the 'Grand Passion' among others, so the love-letters, which cover a period of about two months, are a peculiar mixture of proposition, over-organization (for both achieved petty assignation and projected lifelong liaison), mushy Victorian Platonism and rather amateurish medical advice. Chapman was convinced that a regimen of water-cures and temperate habit would set right the irregularity of Barbara's 'flow':

> the hip-bath of water at 96 or 98 of temperature rendered pungent with mustard ... Cover yourself with a blanket while in the bath ... Have a supply of *hot* water by you, so that you can prevent the bath from becoming lower than 96 all the time you are in it ... Continue this bath *every* night, until the flow appears. Each morning have a vessel of boiling water brought

into your room and sit over it so as to let it act as a local vapour bath ... Get the horsehair socks *at once* ... Get yourself some large or loose-fitting lambs-wool socks to sleep in, so that your feet may be warm at night ... Coming through Cheapside I found some socks, and *felt* boots which I designed to try for ... You will find them very warm having a hair sock in each ... Take good care of your inner and outer *woman* as the best way of telling me how much you love me, and of making me happy ... The feeling of weight on the head ought to be relieved at once. Purgatives (the pills I prescribe) may do this ... [Dr Williams] is very urgent in recommending what he calls a 'Chamber Horse'. It is a sort of chair, elastic with air, in which you move up and down and which he says has a more direct mechanical action on the womb than has any other exercise. This seems impracticable unless you were fixed in one place ... Avoid cold water as you would the devil ... I am completely obfuscated by your health report: You told me that you became or began to be 'unwell' the 29th of August, and yet you say, in answer to my question – When did the flow cease? 'Night of the *24th*,' and you add that you think you began to take the iron [capsules] again 'the 1st of this month'. What do you mean? Please to be very explicit. Are your feet warm all night? Are they cold before breakfast owing to your washing them in cold water?[2]

These business-like admonitions are alternated with conventional Victorian love-rhetoric:

Anxiety itself is transfigured into a calm feeling of duty under the purifying and ennobling influence of your love. I do pray inwardly that I may more and more deserve it ... It is impossible for me to give you any real account of the feelings I experience; they are to myself a mystery and I seem best to understand something of them when I listen to music and the waves breaking on the shore; or when I look on flowers, the glorious moon, and illumined over floating clouds, the distant summer lightning, as it flashed last night, and above all when I gaze on the silent mysterious stars ... I like to think of you as a joyous careless creature rambling about the woods with the abandon of a bird. Oh my love if you have to make money, the spirit of the world will put its cold finger of care upon you.

As the month wears on, still gasping forth prescriptions and sentimentality, Chapman becomes somewhat impatient with the progress of his more clinical remedies and begins to advocate more direct cures.

> I consulted [Dr Williams] . . . as to the effect of marriage; he eagerly jumped at the idea, exclaiming: 'best thing in the world! best thing in the world!' . . . I do strongly hope [Anna Mary Howitt – he had begun to prescribe for her, too] . . . will ere long approach the normal periods again but, alas, nothing but becoming a mother will release her from the *pain* she suffers each time . . . The strongest reason with me is derived from a consideration of your health, and from the conviction of the re-invigorating effects on your system of a fulfilment of love's physical desires . . . If such be the case he [Dr Williams] would order leeches to be applied at the top of the thighs . . . a much more natural healthy and less repugnant method, the cold water system, would be equally or more likely to effect the same end; but our union would be the healthiest and surest means of all . . . What you want is to cause your skin to glow, to make it perform its functions more perfectly, to make the blood vigorously circulate all over your surface . . . If I were with you night and day, I would, by means of wet and dry towels, make every part of your body glow with a rosy hue, and health would soon return to you then, if your simple possession of me did not itself suffice to bring it . . . You cannot do it effectually or with sufficient cupidity alone.

And Chapman has plans. The *Westminster Review* has been disappointing and won't provide what he needs to support his family, his insurance policies *and* a separate establishment for Barbara. Her income (or at least what she tells him her income is) isn't enough; she might take to writing the Art section of the *Westminster*:

> If you knew German you would soon get into the habit of dashing that off without consuming much time. And of course if you liked you might just as well earn that 125 as anyone else. It is much easier to write articles than to get them inserted but in your case you would have an ever ready recipient and adviser . . . I have promised to show a rich Mr. Ramsay . . . some of your drawings.

And about those drawings:

> You seem to me scarcely ambitious enough. I should like to see you take larger subjects – wider views – to paint larger pictures, and to finish them as highly as you can.

He looks at the situation objectively and decides that, barring unforeseen good fortune, they should be able to begin a separate extramarital establishment by 1856 or 1857 ('1857 seems a long way off'), but perhaps it could be sooner if he could only find the means to complete his medical education by getting rid of 'the business' and attending the requisite lectures, for which he sends her a list and the costs.

One wonders how so intelligent a woman could put up with this. He *was* known in his youth as 'Byron' because of his resemblance to the poet's portraits, but still. It is to Barbara's credit that the reader of the letters can sense a diminishing enthusiasm at that missing end of the correspondence. She takes the plan seriously because she finds it attractive: it's a way around the slavery of marriage. But she shows distinct signs that she is getting fed up with planning and replanning, remedy and gush:

> Never mind the 'Master Passion'; you will not always have a horror of it . . . I was pained by the words – 'Accursed love,' – if you had been well I should have written you a reproof . . . I do indeed repent bitterly of my folly and selfishness last week; and am very grateful to you for not keeping from me that my accursed letters made you ill. Bless you, bless you – I will still try to act as I ought to do.

Several times she seems to have raised the question of what kind of damage all this clinical, sentimental and economic advice was doing to her image of herself as a woman: was there a difference, after all, between the angel at the hearth and the angel waiting at Brighton for the 4.37?

> I see how the old falsehood clings to you. 'You think I shall lose something womanly by struggling for money.' Darling, you are utterly mistaken. I do not think that in struggling for money you would lose something *womanly* but something *human*. I make no distinction of sex in this matter.

Finally, after a number of ultimatums of 'but two alternatives', 'five alternatives', propositions, ways of breaking it to Pater, the plans reach a crisis. Chapman tries to frame a letter she can read to her father (which she will first correct, return – presumably in an envelope addressed by Miss Howitt – and he will copy over for the presentation), but it doesn't work out quite the way it should.

> I commenced a letter ... I scarcely knew what to say, and am by no means confident that what I have written – amid incessant interruptions, and in a kind of anxious excitement, is at all suitable for the object in view.

Pater says no. Chapman tries not to let this discourage him.

> You must *make frequent, very frequent* occasions for discussing the subject with him; he must know all: he must appreciate the real state of your health; what you have suffered; what you will suffer, and how your mind is destroying your body by this terrible contest. The more you talk to him, the more he will become enlightened, the more he will be enabled to perceive the conditions of your welfare and the vainness of any resolve that we shall *live* apart ... Yours until death, J.C.

The correspondence breaks off, and Barbara is trundled off with her sisters by her brother Ben to Algeria and into the arms, as it turns out, of Eugène Bodichon.

One might better have predicted that Barbara's father would have accepted the idea of a lifelong extramarital liaison for his daughter. Benjamin Smith was a radical, an active Liberal M.P. and Anti-Corn Law politician from a long radical line, and had never separated his politics from his social behaviour or his family. The Smith family had taken the side of the Colonists in the American revolution – no empty political gesture because they gave up extensive land holdings in Savannah, Georgia, to enforce their sentiments. His own domestic arrangement had been extramarital: he seduced a milliner, fathered five children upon her (of whom Barbara was the oldest) and never married. The common-law widower and the children now grown were known to George Eliot as 'the *tabooed* family', partly because of illegitimacy, but surely also because of Benjamin Smith's lifelong radicalism.

He believed women – his daughters, at any rate – should have 'the wind in their sails' and the potential for independent lives, and had settled £300 a year upon Barbara when she came of age. Before his death she had perhaps £1,000 a year, as did her sisters. But perhaps this unorthodox, rather quixotic or even Jamesian theory (now and again one thinks of Isabel Archer in connection with Barbara) of equality and independence was less strong than old-fashioned fatherly feelings when it came right down to the Chapman question. When Barbara had first discussed the projected arrangement in rather general terms, he had suggested that she go to America to practice free love, but perhaps Brighton was just too close for his fatherly pride – or maybe he just didn't like Chapman. What father could? – especially if Barbara had shown him any of those letters, and this would be just what she might have done. In any event, the three sisters were packed off to Algeria, Bella (Isabella) for her consumptive symptoms, Nanny (Anne) for company and Barbara – either as her biographer reports, because 'with the prophylactic of composure gone, the germs of physical disease had an easy prey'[3] or for traditional Victorian reasons – to forget Chapman.[4]

In any event, it was into the arms of Dr Bodichon. When George Henry Lewes heard of her intended marriage, he allowed that it 'made us feel not quite satisfied'. Why? Yes he was an intellectual but no he wasn't good enough for one so good? Yes he was a wonderful man but wasn't he rather *strange*? Most of Barbara's friends responded with misgivings and uncertainty. The prospect of a woman with 'the wind in her sails' raises such uncertainty: will she live up to it? Won't she slip and go too far too soon? It is the perfect situation for the novelist.

But perhaps not the biographer. The Bodichons seem from the evidence of this journal to have been perfectly suited. They went much their separate ways and each pursued his own interests, joining for society or for friends they could hold in common. The Doctor's 'codfish aristocracy' and perhaps some of the endless fraternity of French doctors in New Orleans were not exactly Barbara's cup of tea, nor her mulatto families and black preachers his, but there is a mutuality, very clear in Barbara's journal, which combined disparate interests into a whole.

The trip begins before the journal starts, with a landing in New York, a trip overland by train as far as Ohio, then aboard a steamboat (perhaps at Cincinnati) for the trip down the Ohio and Mississippi. They planned for a somewhat extended

PLATE 1

Barbara Leigh Smith Bodichon

stay in New Orleans and spent even longer. Providing evidence of conventional femininity in the midst of her feminism, Barbara restrains herself from saying how filthy she finds New Orleans until they are well out of it. They proceed by boat and rail north through Mobile, Montgomery (Alabama), Savannah (Georgia), Wilmington (North Carolina), Washington, Philadelphia and Perth Amboy (New Jersey) to the *de rigueur* visit to Niagara Falls before the last leg to Boston and New York for the return to England in June 1858.

Barbara's experiences in America are a microcosm of the concerns of her life and her life is dominated by concerns. They consume most of her energy, her sympathy and her industry and make her life a most consistent whole: she is the same early and late, happy and sad, in liaison and marriage, as philanthropist and friend. She pursues Women's Rights in lectures, through acquaintances among the American pioneers, in conversation, in the arguments of her journal. She spends little time bewailing the evil of slavery – that is a given. She is already thinking about the next step, the rehabilitation of the blacks once emancipation comes – the schools, churches, social barriers which they will face. She tells people what she thinks, early and late, and she watches, looks, sees, investigates with a woman's, a painter's, a zealot's eye. But she is first of all a woman and her concerns all emanate from that core.

Her femininity – an essential part of her feminism – is parallel to that of a very different woman, her close friend, George Eliot. That they were friends is more than just an indication of how bright or attractive in mind and spirit Barbara was, or of how she stood in intellectual society. The friendship is much more than a literary anecdote: it is a framework for comparison. Hester Burton suggests rightly that Barbara was *L'Allegro* to Marian's *Il Penseroso*, but articulate details yield more understanding than generalization, however powerful.

Bessie Parkes introduced Barbara to Marian Evans at one of the Chapmans' 'evenings'. Marian knew she was of the '*tabooed* family' but this seems only to have piqued her interest:

Tell your noble-looking Barbara – I cannot call her Miss Smith, at least to you – that I only hope she will keep up her desire to make an 'indelible impression' on me. It will be no hard task. The material she has to work on is very impressible and I am sure the mould is first-rate.

There was a desire for friendship on either side, but the intimacy which developed is still remarkable, considering the one woman's rage for privacy and the other's drive for public impact. Desire for friendship was augmented most clearly by a quick sense in each of what the other was all about, a quick sense best indicated in the exchange on *Adam Bede*. Barbara was the first to recognize its author, even before she read the book.

My darling Marian!

Forgive me for being so very affectionate but I am so intensely delighted at your success. I have just got the 'Times' of April 12th with the glorious review of 'Adam Bede' and a few days ago I read the 'Westminster Review' article. I can't tell you how I triumphed in the triumph you have made. It is so great a one. Now you see I have not yet got the book but I *know* that it is you. There are some weeks passed since in an obscure paper I saw the 1st review and read one long extract which instantly made me internally exclaim that is written by Marian Evans, there is her great big head and heart and her wise wide views.

Now the more I get of the book the more certain I am, not because it is like what you have written before but because it is like what I see in you. 'It is an opinion which fire cannot melt out of me. I would die in it at the stake.' I have not breathed a word to a soul except to the Doctor who is like the tomb for a secret . . .

I can't tell you, my dear George Eliot, how enchanted I am. Very few things could have given me so much pleasure.

1st. That a woman should write a wise and *humourous* book which should take a place by Thackeray.

2nd. That YOU *that you* whom they spit at should do it!

I am so enchanted so glad with the good and bad of me! both glad – angel and devil both triumph!

Everybody (but Bessie and my Doctor) have bullied me for saying 'My friend Marian' so you see I may take a little pet bit of delight to myself that you will be what all will wish to claim as 'my friend Marian'!

This is only to tell you how I rejoice with you.

B.L.S.B.

There was a strong potential kinship in both Barbara's and Marian's sense of being 'outside' society – the one by virtue of her extramarital liaison, the other perhaps for her illegitimacy or unorthodoxy or independence. Marian's reply reciprocated Barbara's quickness and immediacy. She was amazed and a little alarmed at 'the first heart that has recognized me in a book which has come from my heart of hearts', and cautioned Barbara to keep the secret. 'Your letter today gave me more joy – more heart-glow, than all the letters or reviews or the other testimonies of success', and George Henry Lewes added, 'You're a darling, and I have always said so! . . . You are *the* person on whose sympathy we both counted.'

Barbara was the physical model for Eliot's *Romola*, but more important than that anecdotal connection is the way Barbara recalls the spiritual strength of several of Eliot's heroines. This must have been the chief secret to her remarkable prescience about her friend's fiction. She was one of the few to anticipate that tragedy was coming at the end of *Middlemarch* while still reading earlier parts. She saw Eliot's novels for what they were – something more than the books she wrote, an extension of her life and of her womanhood.

> I do not like the cover [of *Middlemarch*] at all, it is not artistic enough – much better have nothing on the cover than that riggle and landscape, which are not worthy of your work at all. The green is not a bad colour, much better than the blue of the Spanish Gypsy, which was very hard wicked blue and made me unhappy, and a plain Roman letter on that green would have been very nice. Do not let them do what they like in dressing your children it does make a difference and I like to see your things in becoming clothes.

On her side Marian and Lewes attempted to help Barbara and the Doctor to secure publishers for their articles and books. One such attempt was made for the manuscript of the American diary. Barbara sent it to the Leweses on 30 June 1859 and Marian returned it on 23 July. Lewes gave her advice on which publisher (Chapman and Hall) and what approach to use. The publishers replied that the letters were possibly publishable but would first have to be weeded of 'offensive Yankeeisms'. Nanny and Adelaide Procter apparently undertook the revision, but nothing seems to have come of it.

As seen in her recognition of *Bede*'s authorship and in Marian's and Lewes's joint sense of this as an expression of love, a strong impetus to intimacy was Barbara's acceptance, without any fuss at all, of Marian's union with Lewes. She wrote to Bessie Parkes:

> I have quite revised [my view of Lewes]. Like you, I thought him an extremely sensual man. Marian tells me that in their intimate marital relationship he is unsensual, extremely considerate. His manner to her is delightful. It is plain to me that he makes her extremely happy.

They had evidently talked not only of the marital relationship but of whatever form of birth control she and Lewes practiced. Marian returned this in her reaction to the Doctor. Only to Barbara did Marian complain about the 'faults of a friend whose good qualities are made the more sacred by the endurance his lot has in many ways demanded' (she later regretted this and was visited by 'compunction and self-disgust'). After Lewes's death she wrote to Barbara, 'As soon as I feel able to see anybody I will see *you*'. Barbara was one of five friends to whom she revealed her plans to marry Johnny Cross (in a letter which was accidentally not sent), but even without receiving the letter, Barbara was immediate in sympathy and sure in sense:

> My dear I hope and I think you will [be] happy. Tell Johnny Cross I should have done exactly what he has done if you would have let me and I had been a man. You see I know all love is so different that I do not see it unnatural to love in new ways – not to be unfaithful to any memory.

Marian replied that she had been sure Barbara would require 'the least explanation on the subject . . . would spontaneously understand our marriage'.

Friendship between feminists was not only immediate, but seems actually to have gone deeper than other friendships between women, and both Marian Evans and Barbara Bodichon were feminists, in very different ways. Marian would send opinions and sometimes even sign petitions and admired Barbara's activism ('One always gets good from Barbara's healthy practical life'), but as she said at the end of a thoughtful paragraph on female education:

> There are many points of this kind that want being urged, but they do not come well from me, and I never like to be quoted in any way on this subject. But I will talk to you some day, and ask you to prevail on Miss Davies to write a little book which is much wanted.

The veil of her fiction, her temporary incognito, her privacy were violated by the kind of public testimony on which Barbara thrived. Barbara had once, very early, thought of writing a novel. She would almost certainly have written a wretched novel, setting forth good and bad directly in characters, their speeches full of opinion and push. But in the world of action – small and large, familial and public – she felt very much at home. Although they did not always agree on the label for the cause, they were united in improving the lot of women, and this companionship gave yet another impetus to intimacy. The large amount of rather sentimental 'soul-kinship' professed by female friends in the nineteenth century – like nothing so much as some of John Chapman's fatuous platitudes – should not prejudice our reading of this affectionate friendship. Both were outsiders, one public and the other private, both near-spinsters, one oddly marital and the other connubially extramarital, both were activists, one incarnating her causes in the other world of fiction, the other pursuing small concerns to a great end. Each was like and quite opposite to, the other; each envied but escaped the other's fate. As in the friendship of Henry James and Robert Louis Stevenson, each envied the other's gift and heaved a sigh of relief as he realized it could never be his.

At first glance, Barbara can look like the stock figure of the nineteenth-century woman and she could have become just that. She painted: what better polite art for a Victorian than dabbling in watercolours. But the quick impression proves false. She studied with William Henry Hunt and Corot, had been taken to Turner's studio – privileges which her father's money or her grandfather's connections could have bought. But she also attracted the admiring comment of John Ruskin and Dante Gabriel Rossetti's praise in his *catalogue raisonnée* of the 'British Exhibition'. She had two shows at the French Gallery in London, in 1859 and 1861. The *Athenaeum* (which could be less than polite, especially about polite ladies' art) was more than polite about the 1861 showing, which included some paintings from her American tour.

> Forty-three drawings of mark. The subjects are mainly found in Algeria, and for powerful rendering of peculiar atmospheric effect, the transcripts from them are eminently successful; they present to us a climatic character always to be found faithfully rendered in this lady's drawings . . . a truthfulness and consistency of expression which indicate their complete fidelity . . . *A Swamp near New Orleans*; we have palms that droop their many-leaved arms in the sluggish and purple river; the mosses that hang about like flags torn in battle; and the gaunt cypresses looking gloomily on. The whole scene is desolate, aguish and still.

One of Marian's painter friends, F. W. Burton, expressed admiration: 'Didn't care about the want of finish in some of them – they had finer qualities than that of finish – he felt they were done on the spot under true inspiration.'

Into Rossetti's admiration crept just a note of simple affection: he liked the woman.

> Ah if you [Christina] were only like Miss Barbara Smith! a young lady I meet at the Howitts', blessed with large rations of tin, fat, enthusiasm, and golden hair, who thinks nothing of climbing up a mountain in breeches, or wading through a stream in none, in the sacred name of pigment. Last night she invited us all to lunch with her on Sunday; and perhaps I shall go, as she is quite a *jolly fellow*.

The 'tin' Barbara had – by this time in excess of £1,000 a year – must be taken into account in many of her friendships, and certainly in Rossetti's. She supported all sorts of educational ventures and he probably looked to her for support of some of his projects in the future. She gave him and Robert James Stillman (mentioned in the American journal) the use of her cottage at Scalands in the spring of 1870 when Elizabeth Siddall was in poor health. The cottage had some hallmarks of wealth:

> In the openings are various kennels of pointers, retrievers, and beagles, which are used in the shooting season by Madame

Bodichon's brothers and brother-in-law, General Ludlow [Bella's husband]. They give us plenty of dog music.

Rossetti, none the less, saw through this to some Bodichon peculiarities:

> Barbara does not indulge in bell-pulls, hardly in servants to summon thereby – so I have brought my own. What she does affect is any amount of thorough draught – a library bearing the stern stamp of 'Bodichon', and a kettleholder with the uncompromising initials B.B. She is the best of women.

Had she been born fifty years earlier, Barbara might have been forced to be content with the intellectual zeal of a blue-stocking, reading the new books, having exciting conversations perhaps even an intrigue or two, but never really *doing* anything. But the dawning independence of the time, together with the freedom provided by her father and the enlightened traditions of her family, had given free rein where containment and frustration would almost certainly have been the rule earlier. Even with her independence, the course for 'proper' indulgence in action was clear: painting – or the Portfolio Club she, her sisters, Anna Mary Howitt and Bessie Parkes and others had formed at which they presented drawings and poems on a theme designated for each meeting. Had she stuck to it, this would have been within the contemporary measure for 'correct' activity. Or she could have run off on the much-travelled road to Rome:

> Nanny wants religion with forms and ceremonies, something present, something of routine, and how many do want it! and what is to give it them? ... Now don't think I am going over with Bessie to the C. C. but I do see that the 'golden rule' and the matins and vespers she attends do her daily good, make her more cheerful and bright ... We talk very much of all the bearings of this question. B's great argument is what I wish for, that liberty, order, justice for all, and succour for the sick and poor is better supplied to the world by the CC than by any other organization. I don't agree to the argument; 1st if it is true of the past or present, it is no reason why it should be true in the future, and I deny that it is true.

Spiritualism too could have satisfied a proper Portfolio-Club Barbara, but Barbara as she was investigated and rejected it in very short order.

> S[tillman] says that Mrs. B[odichon] has no definite belief in or opinion about the existence of the disembodied soul. Her husband, who remains in Algeria, is wholly given up now to spiritualism – which she flouts.

As William Michael Rossetti observed, 'Mrs. Bodichon was sceptical about more things than one – spiritualism was one of them', even after the Doctor 'took very much' to it 'after a certain date'.

Things to be interested in were not the same as what had to be done, and in 'this God's world', there was plenty that had to be done. Feminist agitation was considered a threat in England at mid-century even before it had been judged a joke in the States. England had a woman on the throne who viewed with qualified distaste her own role in government ('We women are not *made* for governing – and if we are good women, we must dislike these masculine occupations...') and viewed with alarm the aspirations of her female subjects to take on even the most minor role.

> The Queen is most anxious to enlist every one who can speak or write to join in checking this mad, wicked folly of 'Woman's Rights', with all its attendant horrors, on which her poor feeble sex is bent . . . It is a subject which makes the Queen so furious that she cannot contain herself . . . Woman would become the most hateful, heartless, and disgusting of human beings were she allowed to unsex herself . . . The Queen is sure that Mrs. Martin agrees with her.

A Mrs Schunck wrote to Henry Crabb Robinson of one feminist meeting, expressing the usual shock and dismay at the 'Doctoresses', one 'dressed in gentleman's clothes'.

> Then there was a Madame Bodichon, the wife of a French physician residing at Algiers. She also read a paper: when young she was very beautiful and full of talents – a Miss Barbara Smith, the illegitimate daughter of a Mr. Smith and a great friend of Miss Bayley . . . Miss Be[ssie] Park[e]s . . . made herself rather conspicuous by her flowing hair, like a little child's of seven years old. What would our great-grandmothers say to such doings?

Probably Barbara would have been content to have had her illegitimacy bandied about as long as she could be assured that her great-grandmother would disapprove. But ancestral disapproval was like the Portfolio Club – no substitute for accomplishment. Barbara's feminism was not protest for the sake of outrage but the essential first step to accomplishment.

In 1854, aroused by the case of Mrs Caroline Norton, Barbara drew up and published *A Brief Summary, in Plain Language, of the Most Important Laws concerning Women.* It apparently found its audience because it went into a second edition in 1856. Through Matthew Davenport Hill, Q.C., the Law Amendment Society was induced the same year to consider the position of married women, and a ladies' committee was formed for which Barbara drew up the petition, presented to Parliament on 14 March with more than 24,000 signatures. The crux was that married women should have a right to their own earnings, 'as a counteractive to wife-beating and other evils'. George Eliot consented to sign and circulated it to some friends.

> That the manifold evils occasioned by the present law, by which the property and earnings of the wife are thrown into the absolute power of the husband ... That if these laws often bear heavily upon women protected by the forethought of their relatives, the social training of their husbands, and the refined customs of the rank to which they belong, how much more unequivocal is the injury sustained by women in the lower classes, for whom no such provision can be made by their parents, who possess no means of appeal to expensive legal protection, and in regard to whom the education of the husband and the habits of his associates offer no moral guarantee for tender consideration of a wife.

The committee included Elizabeth Barrett Browning, Sarianna Browning, Jane Welsh Carlyle, Mary Cowden Clarke, Charlotte Cushman, Mrs Gaskell, Mary and Anna Mary Howitt, Anna Jameson, Harriet Martineau, Bessie Rayner Parkes and Elizabeth Reid. The number of signatures was not remarkable, but the results were: a consciousness that women could do more than sit and wait, and, eventually (although not until 1882) the passage of the Married Women's Property Act, the first concrete breakthrough by the British feminists.

Barbara's father had settled upon her at her majority, together with the independent income, the title-deed to the

Westminster Infant School in Vincent Square. She undertook to reactivate it along new lines. She moved it to Portman Hall (Carlisle Street, Church Street off the Edgware Road) to make it independent of its past and made it into a laboratory for experiment in primary education. Sometimes she and her sisters helped Elizabeth Whitehead with the thirty-six pupils (who paid only 6d. per week). When the school outlived its usefulness in 1864 Barbara gave its equipment to the Working Women's College.

She pursued the feminist cause on several fronts: she sought means to find or create suitable feminine professions so that girls would not have to 'marry – stitch – die – or do worse'. She continued to write – 'Women and Work' (1857), 'Reasons for the Enfranchisement of Women' and 'Objections to the Enfranchisement of Women Considered' (both 1866). She helped found the *Englishwoman's Journal* and published there and elsewhere articles on her American travels and abolition. Still, writing, even writing which advocated activist causes was not really enough. Words were only the earnest of deeds. Unfortunately the way to deeds led through a thicket of committees and societies: the Society for Promoting the Employment of Women, the Middle Class Emigration Society, the Ladies' Institute, the Committee for Obtaining the Admission of Women to University Examinations, the Kensington Society. And Barbara was in demand as much for her money as for her energy and zeal. She saw it quite simply, though: she had the wind in her sails and wanted to help those who did not. Money was:

A power to do good ... a responsibility which we must accept ... if you get money, you gain a power of sending a child to school, of buying a good book to give to the ignorant, of sending a sick person to a good climate.

But with the committees and the societies and the concerns came friends, recruitment – and obligations. She wrote to Marian Evans in 1859:

I am so worried by people and invitations and parties got up for me that I think I shall say I am not married to Dr. Bodichon just to titter the people! they torment me so. You are right to be rid of the world. I know now what your life is worth, having some of it on my hill above the Mediterranean with my Doctor. Sometimes here I get so sick that I think I must run away – I get home sick and love sick and long to be sea sick to get over there again.

Even Algeria was not an escape; she and the Doctor were at work there in campaigns for afforestation and sanitation.

In the midst of social necessities for the cause, she gave casual visitors the bum's rush: 'Devastators of the day, away, away!' she would cry out the door. Emily Davies, agitating for women's university education, sympathized closely with the peculiar obligation of the benefactress:

> People *won't* let her alone. It is quite a caution against forming the habit of benevolence, it is so difficult to break off.

And Miss Davies too felt the drain of the social fringe of societal change and adopted Barbara's solution: Madame Bodichon, she wrote to a friend, 'thinks nobody ought to go to parties who is tired by them. If nobody did, parties would soon come to nothing'. But Barbara's exhaustion went deeper, too, to the discouragement and frustration of re-starting, re-climbing, urging on those whose zeal didn't match hers. She wrote to William Allingham in 1862:

> I confess the enthusiasm with which I used to leave my easel and go to teach at the school or help Bessie in her affairs is wearing off, and if it were not that at thirty-five one has acquired habits which happily cannot be broken, I should not go on as I do; I could not *begin* as I used ten years ago at any of these dusty, dirty attempts to help one's poor fellow-creatures, and it is quite natural that my life abroad and out of doors should make me more enterprising for boar-hunts or painting excursions, than for long sojourns in stifling rooms with miserable people. I think of the 'Palace of Art' and know it is my temptation.

But if the dream of that poem was her temptation, bringing down to earth Tennyson's dream of the female academy in *The Princess* was to be her lot. Her most significant accomplishment was to be her role in making possible English university education for women.

Tennyson's own view of Women's Rights was closer to the unreconstructed norm than the zealous forefront. Jane Welsh Carlyle observed of him:

Alfred is dreadfully embarrassed with women alone – for he entertains at one and the same moment a feeling of almost adoration for them, and an ineffable contempt! Adoration, I suppose, for what they *might be* – contempt for what they *are*!

This was what Barbara and Emily Davies were up against. One of the opponents to Barbara's committee seeking to obtain the admission of women to the university examinations, quite seriously, held that the difference between the male and the female mental organization was that it was the function of men to accumulate wealth and that of women to distribute it. A woman in a university was an absurdity.

But Emily Davies, Barbara and a few others thought not. Miss Davies could not be persuaded to take an active role in the campaign for enfranchisement but from the beginning saw university education as a means of raising women to a publicly accepted equality, leading in turn to enfranchisement and other rights. Barbara confessed that she had dreamed of women's university education ever since she had visited her brother Ben at Jesus. Davies was the leader and Barbara was her supporter: she felt she did not 'deserve to be called the originator of the college' and 'certainly could not have carried out the plan as Miss Davies has done'. But she could function on committees, talk people into serving in various ways, into relaxing statutes a little bit so that an examination could be given and, as always, could give, as Rossetti put it, some of her 'large rations of tin'. She gave £1,000 in 1867 and enlisted Marian Evans for £50 (designated as 'from the author of *Romola*').

She had disagreements with the foundress along the way: Barbara felt that it was a mistake to start up the operation anywhere but Cambridge proper and Miss Davies elected to hire a house at Hitchin. After Miss Davies had won that battle first and Barbara had won it later (when the Hitchin operation was moved to Girton in 1873), Miss Davies became annoyed at the self-effacement of some of Barbara's gifts – it was clearly confusing.

I did not know you meant the book case for the Mistress's room ... I suppose your chairs are for the *College*. If you use that vicious expression 'for you' again, I shall keep the things for myself.

But most of the enterprise was, again, a happy congruence of women in a common cause. The college was in most respects beginning from the ground up and, although its founders were generally cautious about distinctions between male and female minds and suspicious of programmes 'especially suited to the woman's needs', there were nevertheless distinctions which had to be made. One wrote:

> Is there no euphonious feminine to be discovered of one of all these names – Rector, Warden, Provost, etc., which prevail at Oxford? ... Dean *has* a feminine in Spanish, but alas, it is duenna.

They wisely settled upon Mistress, in conformity with Cambridge custom.

Barbara sent drawings for the public rooms, visited and encouraged, corresponded to raise money, got Marian to give books, offered Blandford Square for examinations in London, and Miss Davies felt free to call upon her in a crisis. The girls in 1871 took it into their heads to have a play at the college, precipitating the 'acting crisis' and Barbara was called in. She spoke sternly against this 'spirit of revolt', and against the shameful practice of the girls taking men's roles and dressing in male costume, but in the midst of one such diatribe her theoretical assurance collapsed completely. The student later reported that Madame Bodichon had come 'to curse and remained to bless' because in the middle of her attack on the costumes she had spotted in the corner of the room a new sort of mourning frock the girl had designed along simple lines something like a cassock, and wanted one for herself.

Her health was by this time failing sharply. Ever since before Chapman it had been a continual cause for concern to her family and friends (which explains the many assurances in this journal that Doctor is taking good care of her in America). Weak lungs, 'Algerian fever' in 1867, nervous irritability extending to 'fetters on her speech' and in 1877 an attack of 'aphasia and other symptoms of nervous weakness' were all maddening drains on a woman who needed energy in order to be characteristic, in order to push her concerns, to get things done. But now her mobility was limited. She could no longer go to Algeria for the winter, and the Doctor on his side of the ocean was kept from coming to England (his last visit was in 1880) and had perhaps gone a bit strange. He died there in 1885, deep in spiritualism. Barbara was bound to Scalands, painting a little bit every day and visiting with those friends who could come to call.

Before her death in 1891 she had given to Girton one sum of £5,000 (retaining a life-right to £250 per year) and at her death willed her savings (her inheritance, she felt, had to go to the family) of £10,000 to the College. The College was on its way and women had passed another milestone on the long path of which she had known so much.

At one point when crusading in support of John Stuart Mill, the new M.P. for Westminster, Barbara had turned to Emily Davies and uttered prophecy: 'You will go up to vote upon crutches, and I shall come out of my grave and vote in my winding sheet'. She did not underestimate the natural conservative resistance of parliament and people, only her friend's stamina: Miss Davies walked to the polls in 1919 at the age of eighty-eight.

NOTES

Most of this introduction is based upon Gordon Haight's studies of George Eliot (*Letters*, 7 vols, 1954–5; *George Eliot and John Chapman*, 1940; *George Eliot, a Biography*, 1968); Hester Burton's biography, *Barbara Bodichon*, 1949; and Barbara Stephen's *Emily Davies and Girton College*, 1927. Passages from the Chapman-Bodichon correspondence, for the most part published here for the first time, are used by permission of the Beinecke Rare Book and Manuscript Library, Yale.

1 The quotations from the letters are taken from a typewritten transcript made for Clement Shorter about 1915. Shorter apparently planned to write a biography of Chapman: the volume containing the transcript also includes a partial transcript of Chapman's diaries for 1851 and 1860 and newspaper clippings.

2 Later when he had become an M.D., 'Licentiate of the Royal College of Physicians', his faith in temperature remedies got him into some trouble when he asserted their efficacy in the treatment of diarrhoea, epilepsy, paralysis, diabetes and cholera.

3 Hester Burton (1949) sees the trip as an attempt to rid Barbara of

the 'weakness' of 1854, the same symptoms Chapman was attempting to remedy. But she never mentions Barbara's affair with Chapman.
4 Gordon Haight suspects that Ben was instrumental in breaking up the Chapman affair. In Chapman, diary for 5 March 1860, is found: 'Sir George and Lady Grey and *Ben*. Smith (!) were there. Of course I never spoke with the latter.'

CHAPTER III

AN AMERICAN DIARY
1857–8

[On the Mississippi River aboard the steamer *Baltic*]
Sunday, 6 December.[1]

I had no time to tell you of my long conversation with the Hon^able——,[2] one of the representatives of Kentucky and his daughter. I had a note to him and gave it to him in the coach coming from the cave where I met him. He was a fine fellow, tall and strong like all these Kentuckians, but so strangely ignorant of the commonest things. He asked me the hours of House of Commons sittings. I said from seven or eight o'clock a.m. to twelve or one a.m. He turned round and said to his daughter Juliet, 'You know when the lady says seven, that is not the same as seven with us; it is a great deal earlier in the day because the sun sets earlier by some hours,' and I could not make him understand it was the same as seven with them! Miss Juliet was a specimen of a Southern lady. She could not travel alone; she was pale and looked dissipated. She had been brought up in the Great Convent at Washington[3] where fashionable Southerners go for education and where they are worked so hard that (she said) all had complexions like hers after a year of school. I never heard of a worse system of education in my life, and, according to her account, the girls were as bad as the system – intriguing, lying creatures. – Miss Juliet told stories of the way in which lovers were got into the convent in disguise, and this before three young men in the coach who very much admired her conversation. She was a horrid animal. She told me her mother was married at thirteen and her sister at fifteen and says it is custom in the Slave States. So Mrs. P. said; she herself was married at fifteen and her husband's first wife was fifteen. Miss Juliet could not walk a mile, says few South state American women can; so say all the ladies here in the boat. Slavery makes all labour dishonourable and walking gets to be thought a labour, an exertion.

There are a dozen black women on the boat – one free and one working for her freedom. Her master will sell her to herself for $300 (very cheap – £60) and she has only $80 more to get. She is born of a father and mother who were brought from Africa – this is rather rare to find, I believe. She is very hideous, very black, and looks very low in the human scale, yet she has the strongest desire for liberty.

We came on board on Friday and have only come two hundred miles because we have had fogs, and stood still more than half the time. I do not enjoy this voyage at all. The boat is filled below with horses, mules, cattle, turkeys, chickens, etc., and the smell is horrid. The company, too, is not amusing at all.

Monday, 7 December. Yesterday I was going on to write of a man who makes the voyage very unpleasant, but as I sat writing he passed me very often and looked over me [so] I was afraid. He is mad, but a man of great intellect and wonderful beauty and strength, nearly seven feet high. He has been a Representative, a general in Texas, is a good poet and has an amount of learning quite extraordinary for an American. I know him very well, for ever since we came on board last Friday he has talked, read letters or his own poetry aloud often, to me particularly. He was almost too violent to be agreeable and I got out of his way as much as possible. I was afraid of him after yesterday afternoon. When I was quietly reading Olmsted's book on the South States[4] he comes, flings himself close to by me on the sofa, seizes the book and begins a violent attack on it and the Northerners, then breaks off and says he means to have my jacket, then breaks off and says, 'Your husband is one of those French republicans – hates Louis Napoleon – quite wrong, etc. – there will be a destruction of this boat, your husband will be killed and I shall marry you – whether you like or no.' I was frightened by his violence, but got away quietly and locked myself up in my room and did not go out except with the Doctor.

In the evening Doctor and I were sitting together in the ladies' cabin, where no one has a right to come but the gentlemen belonging to ladies (I forgot to say that this general drinks in the evening and is always worse, but that everyone lets him have his way, and he had been throwing himself on the necks of two or three men, once round the Doctor, which he bore very quietly) – but while we were reading, up rushes the man, mad or drunk, and smashes his hat with great violence on the Dr.'s head who starts up and says he will not be touched by anyone, and if it is attempted again he will defend himself with pistols or cane, and he took the hat and flung it at the General. The General seemed quite cowed and begged the Doctor's pardon, but everyone round interfered and took the General's part and all thought the Doctor's behaviour *very wrong*. I think he was too violent and so in the wrong, but certainly all the rest were in the wrong to take the General's part, and it was entirely because he was an American.

The Captain came and said if pistols were mentioned before ladies he should put the Doctor on shore directly, and – yet his ideas of liberty – allowed a mad man to talk in the most indecent manner before women and risk the lives of all on board, for he might set fire to the boat in an instant. Last week a vessel was set fire to by one person out of spite to some one other on board and *seventy-five people* were burnt or drowned.

This General has been in an asylum but has been sent out *cured* and is alone; it is very likely he was well enough in the House[5] where he could not get rum or whiskey. This is a specimen on a Southern steamboat company. There are other disorderly characters on board. I wish you could have heard the account of an elopement which one of the assistant actors in it gave. He and the lover got into a boarding school and ran off with a young girl into another state, and they were married by a clergyman who asked no questions but charged $100!!!

Tuesday, 8 December. Since I wrote to you I have read in the Louisville paper an account of General Haskell. He seems to be a great genius driven mad with excitements – politics and wine. He seems to be *the man* of Tennessee. They are as proud of him as possible.

We are on the MISSISSIPPI now, it is a magnificent river and the everlasting woods on either side are very striking. We stop very often at little places like this very ugly and queer.
The mistletoe here grows in the trees in immense quantities. I could not think what plant it could be.

The mist often lies on the water in a very beautiful and curious manner but is too like a fever spirit altogether to please me.

We have seen six or seven families in their houses floating down on rafts. It is one of the most curious sights I ever saw in my life. They have an immensely long rudder, no oars, no

2

Tuesday

Since I wrote to you I have read in the
Louisville paper an account of General
Haskell he seems to be a great genius
driven mad with excitements politics
& wine .... He seems to be the man of
Tennessee, they all are proud of him as
possible.

We are on the MISSISSIPPI now, it
is a magnificent river & the everlasting
woods on either side are very striking
We stop very often at little places like
this very ugly & queer.

Blown up steamer

The mistletoe ~~which~~ here growin in the trees in
immense quantities I could not think what
plant it could be.

The mist often lies on the water in a very
beautiful & curious manner but is to
like a fever spirit altogether to please me

We have seen 60 y families in their houses
floating down on rafts it is one of the most
curious sights ever saw in my life
they have are immensely long sudder as oars
on sails they just live quietly with their animals
~~doing~~ their household work every day & at last

sails. They just live quietly with their animals doing their household work every day, and at last finding themselves at their destination without any trouble but that of keeping away from banks and snags.

We pass plots of ground which the Captain says he knows have grown from 60 to 75 bushels of wheat for 57 years, and he knows a man here at Kickman City[6] (which I have drawn) who grew 125 barrels of potatoes on one acre and sold them on the land for one dollar and a half a barrel. He put them into barrels on the land; barrels cost him one quarter of a dollar each.

The banks of the river do really look as if their riches were inexhaustible and yet the beginning of civilization – a log hut, a field of maize with black stumps standing up all over it is very desolate. The monotony of forest at the edge of the water is very fine with certain effects of sky.

Now for the end of General H. He came up to me two nights ago and said in the most eloquent way how sorry he was he had offended the Dr., and would the Dr. shake hands, and would I go and ask him. So I went and the Dr. came up and there was a grand scene. Dr. said, 'I bear no rancour –' 'No, no, let us be friends,' and after they talked and I danced two everlasting cotillions with the General, negroes playing for us. It was great fun, for the music seemed to have the best effect on the General, soothing his mind. It was quite dramatic, that reconciliation. The people round clapped their hands! very unlike the Northerners.

Friday, 11 December.
Baltic Steamer, Mississippi.
Last night I sat finishing up my sketches at the public table. *Company:* the pretty little Mrs. H. and her fair Scotch-looking husband, Mr. C. the intellectual-looking Californian gentleman and Mrs. B. who has a very beautiful expression and is the most refined woman on the boat. Mr. C. is reading a paper and read out loud the announcement of the marriage of a mulatto and a white girl; it excites from all expressions of the utmost disgust and horror. I say, 'It is very uncommon?' Mr. C.: 'Yes! thank God. Only permitted in Massachusetts and a few states.' 'There seems to be nothing disgusting in it.

My brothers went to school with a mulatto and I with a mulatto girl, and I have seen mulattoes in England who were not unlikely to marry with white.' *All:* 'At school! At school with niggers!' 'Yes.' *All:* 'Horrid idea, how could you?' *BLS*: 'Why, your little children all feel it possible to come in close contact with negroes, and they seem to like it; there is no natural antipathy.' *Some:* 'Yes, there is an inborn disgust *which prevents amalgamation.*' (Mark this: only one-half the negroes in the United States are full-blooded Africans – the rest [the] produce of white men and black women.) *Some:* 'No, it is only the effect of education.' *Mr. C.:* 'There is no school or college in the U.S. where negroes could be educated with whites.' *BLS:* 'You are wrong, Sir. At Oberlin men, women and negroes are educated together.'[7] *Mrs. B.:* 'Yes, I know that, because Lucy Stone was educated there with people of colour.' *Mr. C.:* 'Lucy Stone – she is a Woman's Rights woman, and an atheist.[8] All those people are. Have you heard her speak?' *Mrs. B.:* 'Yes, she speaks wonderfully well. She is an elegant orator. I was carried away by her at first. –She said women had a right to vote and all that sort of nonsense.' *Mr. C.:* 'Nonsense indeed! Why, women, if that they have not certain rights are exempt from certain duties.' *Mrs. B.:* 'Oh, yes, certainly Woman's Rights are great rubbish.' There is evidently a feeling that Abolition and Woman's Rights are supported by the same people and same arguments, and that both are allied to atheism – and all these slave owners are very religious people. I wanted the conversation to stick to slavery so I did not answer this argument with the other side which settles that objection. Women perform as great service to the state in bringing citizens into it as men do in preserving their lives. This is women's duty to the state which counterbalances the services men do the state a thousand times. Mr. C. might have said, 'But this very duty incapacitates them for the right of voting and taking part in the governmental concerns of the state.' The answer is, so does the duty of men to fight, to go to sea, to go to distant parts to defend the state. When it does incapacitate them, let it incapacitate them, all men and women. When it does not, *let it not.*[9] To a candid mind it is evident the duties they fulfil to the state are more onerous than those which men fulfil. They make and educate for ten years all the citizens in the state, and they receive no rights for these services!

But to return, I said instantly, 'Do not you think it right to give any education to the negro race?' *Mrs. B.:* 'Oh, yes. Every child should be taught to read the Bible.' *Mrs. H.:* 'I do not think they ought to be taught to read. It makes them unhappy, and all the negroes who run away, you will find, are those who have learnt how to read. I would not teach them to read.' *BLS:* 'But have they not souls and should not they read the Bible.' *Some:* 'Oh, yes, they have souls, but oral instruction is best for them.' *Mrs. B.:* 'No, I do think everyone should be able to read the Bible.' *Mrs. H.:* 'If you teach them to read they *will* run away.' *Mrs. B.* (who lives in Louisville and is evidently very kind to her slaves): 'Well, I say if they will run away, let them.' *Mr. and Mrs. H.* (who, by the bye are bringing south *a woman who leaves a husband and five children behind in Kentucky*): 'Let them run away if they will! Why, every negro would run away if they could – people don't like to lose their servants.' Some said it makes the negroes unhappy to know how to read – what is the use of it to them? They are inferior to the whites and must be so always. *BLS:* 'But you say they improve and are better off every year, and that there is a wonderful difference between the African as he comes from Africa and the African after two or three generations in America. How can you tell where that improvement will stop?' *Mr. C.:* 'Yes, they improve, but that is no reason for giving them *much* instruction and us making them discontented – for they *never will be emancipated. We cannot consent to lose our property.*'

Mrs. B. after some general observations, says, 'Have you read *Uncle Tom*?'[10] I say, 'Yes.' Mrs. B. says, 'If there is a creature living I *hate it is that Mrs. Beecher.*' This was said with an expression of bitter feeling which distorted her good face, and every vestige of humanity disappeared, under the influence of this feeling. She might equal Brooks' 'glorious manifestation against Sumner.'[11] I do not know how other people feel, but I cannot come amongst these people without the perception that every standard of right and wrong is lost, – that they are perverted and degraded by this one falsehood. To live in the belief of a vital falsehood poisons all the springs of life. I feel in England how incapable men and women are of judging rightly on any point when they hold false opinions concerning the rights of one half of the human race.[12]

Some great questions there are which are ever before us. Every hour of the day brings up occasion of action involving these questions, and we have to consider how we shall act and we see what is the result of our action. To hold false ideas on these great questions which are woven in with every-day life perverts, embitters, poisons the souls more than to hold the most monstrously absurd doctrines of religious faith.[13] It is bad enough to believe all will be damned but yourself and a few friends, but to believe a man has a right to hold fellow-men as slaves, to breed slaves – to sell his own children, – this doctrine perverts a man infinitely more, because when a man daily acts a faith it is a very different thing from thinking you believe. Of all who cry 'God condemns you to *eternal* punishment unless you believe certain dogmas,' would thrust you and himself into the fire he believes the good Lord prepares for you. To believe in transubstantiation or the divinity of the Virgin is not so perverting to the mind as to believe that women have no rights to full development of all their faculties and exercise of all their powers, to believe that men have rights over women, and as fathers to exercise those pretended rights over daughters, as husbands exercising those rights over wives. Every day men acting on this false belief destroy their perception of justice, blunt their moral nature, so injure their consciences that they lose the power to perceive the highest and purest attributes of God. Slavery is a greater injustice, but it is allied to the injustice to women so closely that I cannot see one without thinking of the other and feeling how soon slavery would be destroyed if right opinions were entertained upon the other question.

We passed Vicksburg, a prettily situated town on one of the rare hills along this vast Mississippi plain. On a hill close to the town about twenty years ago, ten gamblers were hung by the inhabitants of the place. A gang of gamblers had made the town quite unsafe for honest folk. They corrupted the young, fleeced them and sometimes murdered them, it was supposed. The inhabitants could bear it no longer so they met together and said, 'Leave the town in three days or we hang you.' The gang did not leave, so the townsmen took ten and hung them on that hill (see sketch).[14]

On the opposite side of the river (in Louisiana) is the fighting ground. The laws are severe in Mississippi against duelling, so when a duel is to be fought they go over to Louisiana.[15] I asked the Captain how many duels a year – about one a month, and two or three fatal ones a year. Sometimes they begin with double-barrelled guns loaded with shot, at 100 yards, then go nearer and take pistols, then quite close and pull out their bowie knives.

Very often fathers will go over with their sons – quite boys – to see them fight. 'Why do they fight so much in the South,' I asked, 'as you think the Southerners are so much better than the Northerners?' 'Well I don't know as there is any reason for it – they *are* much better than Northerners. Why, if a beggar asks alms a Northerner will give some cents, and a Southerner will give a quarter of a dollar at least.'

There is a recklessness and carelessness about these Southerners which I did not think the Anglo-Saxon race could attain under any circumstances.

Saturday, 12 December.   Lovely day. We landed in Louisiana and in Mississippi states while the vessel was getting wood. At one place we took a walk for an hour in a wood where all the trees were covered with the grey Spanish moss (not a moss, by the bye, but a parasite, with flower and a pod like a vetch).[16] The effect was strange and beautiful. I enjoyed it more than anything I have seen in America. There are subjects for thousands of pictures. Why should artists born here paint everlasting campagnas, domes and towers? Why, – their forests are a new revelation of nature's beauty. God must have been in an Edgar Poe frame of mind when he thought of throwing this weird grey drapery over their forests. I am bewitched with this new phase of beauty. I never imagined anything like it. Old trees leaning on young trees, the dead prostrate; haughty trees springing straight up to heaven and then spreading out into a fir-like tower – boughs, all of them, covered with this grey garment hanging down straight. Some look like Dante Rossetti's figures – clothes and souls and – nothing more. Sometimes the trees look covered with grey icicles – always beautiful and fantastic, sometimes sublime. How grateful we should be if American artists would send us over some of this curious beauty.

As we were going into this wood we met a negro woman driving a cart. She nodded to me, so I began to talk to her and told her where I came from. 'England! a good country. I guess you won't stay long in this – it is a *mean country*.' 'Why, it is yours, is it not?' 'Mine! thank God, no! – I come from ole Virginny and I would not stay here if I could help it, but we poor coloured people are sent about here and there jist as the white folk please.'

We had moored close by a cotton plantation in the morning and my friends the niggers had been knocking me up to go and see how 'the poor creatures work, like beasts – hundred of 'em and a white overseer.' Dr. B. went out into the field and brought me a branch of the cotton plant and I sat down after breakfast in the cabin to draw it. Mr. Collins the Californian gentleman comes and sits by me and says, 'I wish you, Madam, would write a book on America. You are more candid and cool in your judgments than any English travellers I have met. You will give a fair picture of slavery. It is no evil – very far from it – quite a blessing for the African' etc. Another gentleman chimed in, 'I have lived all my life in the slave states and I assure you, slavery is a good institution.' They both went on to say it was very rarely that families were separated, etc. They begged of me to write a fair view of the case.

I assured them I should not write a book on America, and that though I could not say anything about the state of the slave I could say that the principle was unjust and every slave had a right to run away, etc. And I went into my cabin and found Polly there, the black (real black) I mentioned before. I said, 'Polly, how many times have you been sold?' 'Twice.' 'Have you any children?' 'I had three. God only knows where two of them are. My master sold them. We lived in Kentucky. – One – my darling – he sold south. She is in one of these fields perhaps picking with those poor creatures you saw. – Oh dear, Mum, we poor creatures have need to believe in God, for if God Almighty will not be good to us some day, why were we born? When I heard of his delivering his people from bondage I know it means the poor African.' Her voice was so husky I could hardly understand her, but it seems her master promised to keep one child and then sold it without telling her and when she asked in agony, '*Where is my child?*' the master said, 'Hired out,' – but it never came back. I found she was a member of the church I visited in Louisville.[17]– She said to me on parting, 'Never forget me. Never forget what we suffer. Do all you can to alter it.'

A free mulatto, a very intelligent man, told me some things too horrible to write. He was a sort of upper waiter over all the rest and much trusted by the Captain. His father was his master. He had bought himself of his own father.

He told me there was no career for free negroes, no rights, no public position. All he said might have been said by any woman anywhere.

I find Mrs. B. is divorced from her husband and is Miss Sophia Titney.[18] In Kentucky divorce is easy – for adultery, for cruelty, for desertion, for slander, or even public ridicule or intoxication. I believe Mrs. B. obtained her divorce on the grounds that her husband had held her up to public ridicule by publishing certain private letters of hers against her wishes.[19] There was a good deal of conversation about her as she was the most interesting woman on board and sang very sweetly. The gentlemen all said she would marry again and that no man would think the divorce any impediment. Mr. Collins said a cousin of his had divorced his wife and both had married again and the husband to a divorced woman. In California divorce is quite easy. I asked over and over again, 'Do you think easy divorce makes married life happier or unhappier than where divorce is impossible?' They all answered happier except one lady who was a Catholic.

21 December.
New Orleans.[20]

My dear Mr. Gratton,[21]

I wish you many happy returns of your birthday! So does the good Doctor, too. If I minded his constant reminders, your birthday could not have passed without a letter – now you will not get this until January 1858, if you get it at all. The fact is I have been so mad with you all in England for not writing to me that I had not the heart to write. I had no letters from anyone for six weeks. Now I know letters have been lost both ways. This American post is the devil. Sometimes they throw out of the train one of the letter bags if they want to take in an extra passenger because the government pays so little for the mails:[22] so they tell me here.

If you were here you would go wild as you did at Algiers with the vegetation and the strange mixture of races of people. There is enough to interest us for a month here so we took two rooms and set up housekeeping (Doctor being the housekeeper because, you see, his work is head work and it is good for him to have a little marketing and house affairs to attend to, and my work is hard head work and hard hand work too, and I can be at it all day long except when I take walks for exercise). You never saw anyone walk as the Doctor does – twenty or thirty miles all over the country. I am a good walker and think little of eight, nine, ten miles, but I can't go the long excursions he does. He walks five and six hours without resting – too much for you, even.

If you were here I would give you a very curious birthday dinner: queer fish, gumbo soup,[23] roast grey squirrel, boiled wildcat, omelette of alligators' eggs, seven fried bananas and cocoanuts – they are so cheap, five or six bananas for $2\frac{1}{2}$d. and a delicious cocoanut for $2\frac{1}{2}$d. We have two date palms in our garden, but I do not fancy they bear fruit here.

This town is much the most amusing American town I have seen. It is so full of strange creatures – Indians, negroes, Spaniards, Germans, Chinese, etc. etc., and all the mixed races. The white people here are pale, thin and wretched looking, the mulatresses and quadroons are fine looking, handsome, tall creatures with splendid eyes. I can't say, generally speaking, there is much beauty in America. They seem to think I am very good looking, which they would not do if they had a high standard of beauty.

Aunty dear: you need not be afraid of the Doctor not taking care of me. He takes the same sort of care of me that Miss Hays used to do at Roughwood, and you said I should not find a husband who would do so. He is something like her in his ways – not so elegant, but more—.[24]

Aunty scoundrel! You have never written one scrap to me all the four months I have been away. Write to me at 79 East

15th St., New York. We shall leave here this day three weeks and go to a place in the neighbourhood on the Mississippi to wait for money because there is something for me to do there. Then in February, shall be at Savannah for one or two months, and work up to Washington for the Spring months, and so north until we come back to you in jolly old England. Eugene's love to Aunty.

Always your affect. Barbara L. S. B.

22 December.
New Orleans.

My dear Aunty,

I can't let your birthday go without a letter and, having sent off a letter to Mr. Gratton this morning shall send this off by the next post. *I hope you will get it.* I did not pay Mr. Gratton's because I thought it safer not, but I shall pay this because I don't think you will find it worth a shilling.

Many happy returns of your birthday. Even if you don't get this in time you won't think I forgot you, because I never forget you and always wish you good things wherever I am.

We have beautiful weather here. I can paint out of doors – forests of oaks draped with the grey moss (a specimen I enclose in this letter) haunted with alligators – these are my subjects. Quite strange – wild, original enough to suit the devil in me.

Studying that alligator almost made me ill – he is so hideously wicked looking. I think of bringing Mr. Gratton an egg: He might hatch it and have a young alligator in the greenhouse. When they come out of the egg (which is the size of a hen's egg but longer) they are eight inches long. They are horrid creatures. The pupil of the eye long [illustration] not round; the lower jaw does not move. You can't imagine anything more fearful than to see them open the upper jaw quite wide. I do wish Mr. Gratton could study the devils with me.

After two hours in company with this demon (I send you) I was obliged to go and refresh myself in the market, where I saw big branches of orange arranged for Xmas and I bought one bough for 2½d. with four oranges on it and a big bundle of radishes. I walked home with them just stopping to look at a mockingbird which I feel rather inclined to buy for you. It is such a dear creature. I saw a parrot, red and blue, walking in a yard where grew magnificent date palm, quite a Southern picture. This is a very pleasant town for a month or two, but it must be horrible in summer – nothing like a hill anywhere. The water in the town runs (when it does) away from the river. The Mississippi is fine to see rushing down at such a rate – eddies, waves, and little whirlpools – I wish you could see it for a minute. Please tell my people I have posted six letters from New Orleans: two to 5 Blandford Square, two to 2 Savile Row, one to John Thornely, one to J. Gratton. I never receive any acknowledgement for any letters, though I have written a bit of journal every day for the sake of you all in England and post a letter to Pater once a week at least (with one exception) since I arrived in New York the 15th of September. If you know that the letters only bore them to read, let me know and I won't trouble myself to write more than 'I am quite well.' Yr. affect. Bar.

Friday, 25 December (Xmas day), 1857.
New Orleans.

Went to the catholic Church. Heard a very beautiful musical service, some women's voices most exquisite. Saw a striking picture: two negro women kneeling, with the red, yellow and black handkerchiefs on their heads (which negresses generally wear here), their faces full of emotion and expression though the features were like Memnon's.[25] Just before them, leaning against a column, an old negro man with white hair, on which (and the column) sunlight was streaming through the coloured glass – ruby, sapphire and emerald. Someone must paint slaves in the Catholic Church at New Orleans.

Dr. and I went to the German graveyard. The bodies of those who can afford it are put in tombs above ground like white coffers; the poorer are put in masses in square brick tombs – all above ground because there is water everywhere below ground. It is the very, very poor who are buried in the ground, or rather mud. I never saw a drearier place in my life. There were hundreds of wreaths, but in spite of that the whole place looked dirty and desolate.

Saturday, 26 December. Went to Slave Auction Rooms.[26] About twenty slaves, men and women, had just been sold.

The auctioneer, Mr. R., came forward to speak to us. A tall, handsome man with blue eyes, long light hair, at first sight a good and clever expression.

We asked some questions. He answered with great politeness, slowly and distinctly, but all lies. He said husbands could not be separated from wives, nor children until twelve from parents, that a slave if ill treated could demand a sale to change his master! So much for the influence of slavery on white men. I gravely asked, keeping up the farce, when the law to prevent separation of husband and wife had passed – was it old? (Slave marriage is not legal). He said, 'Yes, *old*. That is, for America it was passed last year.' (!!!!) 'A *very good law*,' he said.

How our Yankee landlady laughed when I came home and told her. She is no humbug. She says slavery is a good institution, marriage of slaves absurd, and wrong to teach them to read and write.

She says as soon as they know how to read they will rise and kill their masters. She says, 'What's to prevent them when they get intelligent!'

She has owned slaves – is very sorry she sold one (a woman) because she had children very fast. 'I can't think how I could be so stupid as to sell her – I should have made a great deal of money out of her children. She had a child every year – worth a great deal – but my husband had died and I wanted money directly, so I sold them all.' In answer to my questions she said that she thought more than half the negroes in Louisiana are mulattoes. Almost all the white men have two families – a black and a white one. The mulattoes are generally very unhappy. Next door but one are a number of children and a black wife – a few streets off a white family – same father. These children of the black mother have learnt to dance, sing, draw, etc.

A Mr. Robinson here is much blamed for living openly with a black wife, walking in the streets with her on his arm. He is very rich and the white ladies are scandalized – he ought to have a white wife as well, they think.

Sunday, 27 December. Went to the beautiful circular Unitarian church.[27] Music good, sermon better than most average sermons in England – on Progress. We walked to Carrollton[28] through the forest. Saw numbers of men with guns shooting wild ducks and snipes; as usual many negroes who passed us lifting their hats to the Doctor and said, 'Good day, Sar.' They think he is a gentleman of colour. I heard one say so as we passed. We saw a horse with a negro on his back which was one of the most beautiful horses I ever saw – very large, quite young, not broken in, full of fire and intelligence. The negro said he loved him and cleaned him four times a day to make his coat shine. I do like the negroes very much. They always seem happy *when* you speak to them; it is only by questioning that their troubles come out. They look healthy and well clothed here. In fact, comparing the appearance of negroes in New York and New Orleans, there is no doubt – here they are physically better off. I have seen white children nursing black babies many times here.

We saw the sunset over the Mississippi, and as we sat on the bank talked to the men who were on the rafts floating down with produce (apples, potatoes, flour, etc.) from Kentucky and Ohio. Many were Germans and had their families with them. The Germans will save Americans from going to the devil. The Irish are hated here. Dr. Bodichon met a man who has walked through Algeria as a hawker and is here walking, selling eggs. He says the Irish are worse than Arabs and are hated by the French, Americans and Germans equally. Dr. B. is always meeting people he knows here. One, a professor in the College here,[29] called out to him in the street, 'I was speaking of you in a lecture only the other day and here you are!'

We have not given any letters[30] yet but shall perhaps. Drawing and my queer friends in this house are enough for me at present. Besides, we have only two rooms, and it would be awkward to receive people in my bedroom and in the Doctor's we keep wood and all sorts of things. But rooms are very large – five windows and a door into the veranda – so that we do everything in them with windows open (cooking etc.). Doctor cooks little things beautifully.

This is a much better way of life than hotel life for us and does not cost quite half as much.

Allow me to present our inmates. Colonel —— of the police,[31] Mr. and Mrs. Sillery (he is a ruined Englishman, she a merry American who makes dresses), Mr. Harris (railway clerk), my landlady's son and a child adopted by Mrs. Sillery.

Mrs. Sillery is a character. She was rich once, but takes work and poverty kindly. She is one of those women who have no sensibility – lots of kindness, cheerfulness, but no nerves or imagination. She chose to stay in '53 here when the yellow fever was awfully raging.[32] She nursed seven people who had it and saw every day bodies burnt in the streets by the dozen and never felt afraid. She says death makes no impression on her. 'I know my husband will die (he is consumptive), but I don't care . . . I felt my sister's death very much,' and yet she cut off all her hair and wears it at evening parties on her head in grand plaits!

She has taken a great fancy to me and asks me to go to see her mother's plantation for a few days' visit if I 'will so far humiliate myself.' Whether they know you or not, the Americans are always hospitable. It is enough if you are a stranger. This society is just the society I could not get letters to, you see – excelling *queer*, a few grades lower than most travellers see, and (as far as I can judge) very superior to the same class in England in instruction, polish of manners and number of ideas. But it is exceeding difficult to compare classes. This is really a free country in the respect of having no privileged class – excepting the class of white over black. White men are free in America and no mistake! My wonder is great at the marvellous manner in which the country governs itself. I find myself saying continually, 'This is a free country.' One is so little used to freedom, real freedom, even in England that it takes time to understand freedom, to realize it. Nothing sent from upper powers to be worshipped or humbly listened to, no parsons sent by a class of born rulers to preach and lecture to another class born to submit and to pay. No race of men with honours they have not earned and power over others which the others have not consented them! Heavens, what a difference! Here all who hold power are heaved up by the people, of the people. Until I came to America I hardly felt the strange want of rational liberty in England. How came Franklin and Washington to dare to try this huge experiment? Why, because they saw it was *right* and because they saw New England governing herself so gallantly.

I believe one reason why Americans look so careworn is because they all feel so intensely the responsibility of governing the country.

What an incredible amount of humbug there is in England never struck me before. They talk Christianity – all men equal before God – but it is only in the Free States of America that that idea of Christ's about equality is beginning to be understood.

I find Germans are very proud to be Americans and when you say, 'You are German?' they answer in broken English, 'I am American.' So with the French people. This comes of their right to vote.[33] It makes them feel at home, gives them an importance which they probably never had before, makes them respect themselves, gives them a standing which creates a new motive for self-improvement. The effect of right to vote on the people makes me think much of the effect of the right to vote on women – it will do them immense good; just the good it does these poor Germans, used to paternal governments and feudal institutions. American women will not be worth much until they get this right.

I send Bessie[34] (by Mr. Buxton) the deliberations of some of the legislatures on that question. It will not be long before in some states it is granted.[35]

We don't live in a fashionable quarter, but convenient for railway stations, which is what we want. Near us are shops and queer fractioners who do 'bleeding and cup*in*'; down the street is '*A Vital Atomic Institute*' (don't you pity the vitals of the victim who goes into Dr. L—'s door?). Near him is a 'practical paper hanger' (I want to know what a theoretical paper hanger is?). Farther down the street I see TORPEDOES for sale.[36] Many signs are written in German, Spanish, French and English.

I cannot tell you what the thermometer is, but it is so warm we leave our windows open and I sit in the veranda to read the *Waverley*. The wind today is just like the wind of the desert but damper. – It is warmer out door than in.

That awful young fiend of an alligator made me so nervous that I fear I shall not bring you the fearful picture I intended. He was tied down for me to draw and I sat studying him – he looking at me with the vilest demon eyes — and I was thinking the Doctor's ideas that the spirits of animals rose gradually into higher and higher forms until they made the spirit stuff of men. I was thinking what a bad man this devil would make, when suddenly the Doctor went near and the demon darted up to bite him, tumbled over on his back and bit his own tail and screamed like a child. I had enough of him that day.

Friday, 1 January. Walked into the country, north. We found a turtle shell five feet long, a splendid spider (black, white and gold), a golden green lizard. About 4 miles from New Orleans we sat down under an evergreen oak to sketch and then fired at a mark. Dr. shot best today.

Walking home we met dozens of splendid trotting horses drawing those four-wheeled spider carriages, racing always.

In the evening we had a professor to tea and his son, a little fellow who could not speak one word of English. The *chief of the police* came home 'gloriously tight' – Mrs. Sillery said so drunk he never knew next day where he had been!

Sunday, 3 January.
New Orleans.

Look on the map and you will see a railway goes straight north to Vicksburg on the Mississippi, that they call the Jackson line.[37] Mrs. Sillery (the wife of the sick Englishman) said to me yesterday, 'Go with me up the Jackson line to-morrow.' 'I have no money, I can't,' said I, but she said money did not matter. I put up my drawing things and bread and cheese, and lo and behold found myself in the wilds of Louisiana forty miles from New Orleans without paying for my ticket, and Mrs. Sillery did not pay either.

It was curious going through the cypress forests to see the cows, who had taken the railway as a dry bed, leisurely turning off into the swamp. They made us wait sometimes, for although all the American engines have an iron paw to clear the road in front, they generally stop for a cow or a donkey to get out of the way.

Mrs. Sillery flirted with all the gentlemen in true Southern fashion. I looked out of the window and saw wonderful pictures: *immense* trees – looking like the tall oaks in Fontainbleau Forest. I cannot believe they are cypress trees. *They are,*

I know, but it gives no idea of them to say cypress. These trees are deciduous and the cypress an evergreen, you will say.[38] The lovely star-shaped leaves of the gum tree are red as roses now and looked like red flowers. The bamboo is a graceful plant in the jungle of dark vegetation. I never saw it until today here. The magnolia grows forty or fifty feet high, I should guess. Its foliage is wonderfully perfect and rich in colour – but I am so done up with the excitement of the day that I can't write of anything but Mrs. Sillery. She amuses me very much. She is the frankest person I ever saw. She has no high ideal above herself; therefore, being satisfied, she tells you what she does and thinks in the most astounding manner. Most people, I think, are a little anxious to conceal their vices because they hope to amend. Not so with my friend at all.

She is thirty-seven. She is good-looking and in my hat looked quite attractive. I noticed a gentleman speak to her with embarrassment and I asked her why when we were in the wood. She told me he was her first lover, but one day, having a 'flare up' with him, she accepted a Frenchman out of spite. The day was fixed for her marriage and the Frenchman who had hated his rival went and asked him to be groomsman. Old Lover said, 'Yes, if you are going to marry one of the sisters of Ellen.' Frenchman said, 'You will see,' and behold the bride was Ellen. Old Lover did all he could to prevent the marriage but in half an hour it was over, and then Ellen told the Frenchman she loved the old lover and never should love him!

He was enraged and was jealous, and as she said, 'We led a cat-and-dog life for three years and then I got a divorce and my husband *married my sister*!' And soon after, she married Mr. Sillery. She said, 'You know, I don't love him and I should not care if he died. – If I marry again it shall be an American. I have had enough of Englishmen and Frenchmen.'

The frankness of Americans is amazing! This woman slaves at dressmaking, earns money for her husband and nurses him very kindly. Her character has a kind of superficiality which is very American. I never saw anyone like her in my life.

The conductor of the railway put us out at a log-hut station where he said we should be handsomely treated, and so we were. The station-master made a blazing fire in the stove and we made ourselves quite at home.

I sketched the forest and listened to the conversation of the four workmen who were at breakfast on venison and roasted potatoes (smelling exquisitely savoury) and drinking claret, and thought of your friend who went from the Workhouse at R— to America and wrote that she was eating peach jam and washing it down with good brandy. Two of these workmen were Germans, one Italian, one American.

The American was an old man and his present employment coffin-making. He said, 'I made Mr. ——[39] a coffin two weeks ago and yesterday I went to his widow's wedding.' All the gentlemen *approved* of this haste and wished all widows would marry as soon. Mrs. Sillery said she would send them some wives from New Orleans. I said I would send some from England if they would give me an alligator. 'Oh, a thousand alligators for an English wife!' said the handsome young German.

They talked a great deal about their skiffs and scows, best wood to build them of and how to cheat the custom house when registering.[40]

Then the station-master told of all the accidents he had known. How two conductors had been killed in four years.

I should have enjoyed their conversation much more if they had not *all* used such horrible language. Instead of saying, 'Here is the train,' they said, 'Here is the hell train,' and the Germans never opened their mouths without a Goddamn. I felt inclined to tell them the exquisite story of Sidney Smith,[41] but I thought of that good story of Mr. Howells of German stupidity and held my tongue. You remember how S.S. was bored in a coach by the continual swearing of a young gentleman, and how he (S.S.) began 'Once upon a time (fire shovel! sugar tongs! boots!) a king of England (fire shovel! sugar tongs! boots!) gave a great ball – (sugar tongs! fire shovel! boots!) and a lady dropped her garter (sugar tongs! etc.) and the king picked it up (sugar tongs! etc.) and giving it to the lady said by sugar tongs, fire shovels, boots, honi soi qui honi pense.' The young gentleman said 'By God, a very good story – rather old – but what has sugar tongs, fire shovel, boots to do with it? Sidney Smith said, 'Sir, this is my manner of swearing – What has God, devil and hell to do with your conversation?'

We went to pay a visit to the only house, in which were two

or three German families – two pretty German women, two healthy children and at least ten or twelve men. The way to the house was made from the rail by planks from tree to tree. There was no possibility of walking in the swamp. They were very glad to see us and I talked to them in French (they came from near Strasburg). They said they made money and liked the country! I should not! I never saw or imagined a more disagreeable position than to live in a house in a wood from which you could never walk a step. They said there were many large snakes and alligators by the thousand, but it was too cold that day for them to leave the mud. Would we come again and see them?

It was a strange excursion, difficult to describe, but I hope to paint a picture of a runaway slave in these woods: Tragedy. Mrs. Sillery was the comedy, and her dialogues came in as Shakespeare brings in broad fun next to deep solemn scenes. She knew almost every one in the train, having lived on the line and been born in this country and talked to each *après sa manière d'être*.

Monday, 4 January. Rain came down in torrents all last night. Today our street a river.

Tuesday, 5 January. Went to draw at Carrollton with my big drawing hat, etc. Six negro children who were playing stopped, stared and then began to run away, frightened by my appearance. 'I do not eat niggers,' I said – so they came up to me and one said, 'Why, it's a woman!' 'Why do you wear boots?' 'Because it is wet!' 'Why do you wear spectacles?' 'Because I can't see without.' 'Why do you wear a hat?' 'Because I can't carry a parasol!' So we became good friends. They were jolly children, half naked. One was a real little Topsy[42] who sang and danced, and then seized the youngest and screamed to me, 'I'll sell you this child for two dollars.' The poor little thing howled and cried and I gave Topsy a scolding for such a wicked joke.

By and by a black girl came to me to say that her missis wanted me to go and paint in her backyard that she might see what I was at. The dog was chained – would not I come directly? I said *No*. Just imagine the impertinence of Mrs.

Taylor of Carrollton! I saw her looking from the door at me, but it was below her dignity to come and look, and as I was a working woman I was to carry my drawing into her back-yard! I thought of a certain lady of title in England who asked if that young person (A.M.H.)[43] was coming to stay with me again.

[*Wednesday, 6 January*].[44]   A negro woman came and talked to me. She said her master has seventeen men and a great many women and children slaves. She said some masters were cruel – that the lady who lived in a house close by was brutal. She chained her slaves down and ill-treated them in every way. Look at this advertisement in today's (Jan. 6th) paper that proves chains are not uncommon.[45] A young lady (*white*) came out next, from a little house like a bathing machine. She had lost a brother with Walker in Nicaragua.[46] She told me her troubles. She was a nice girl and we became great friends. She said she was afraid of runaway slaves in the woods – was not I? I said no, I should help them. She said she had not thought whether slavery was wrong or not. She was born here. She said she could walk four or five miles but did not know any New Orleans ladies so strong – 'They will not try to walk,' she said. The other American I have met since I left New York who professed to walk five miles called two hundred or three hundred yards half a mile, so I am suspicious now.

My young friend told me she knew a grown woman who had never seen the moss on the trees and did not know what it was. She lived always in the fashionable world of New Orleans. (Perhaps educated at this school. (See no. 2).[47]

Went to Lake Pontchartrain[48] to paint, very lovely indeed today. Sky and sea beautiful blue.

A German railway labourer came and sat by me. He gets forty dollars a month. He does not like America so well as Germany (Saxony), but, 'this is a free country and I have a vote, so I shall stay.'

Thursday, 7 January.   In the afternoon walked with Dr. B. towards Carrollton. Nothing to see but bathing-machine houses. Sat down to rest after two hours walking and drew what was opposite to me: four cows, a negro and a horse, a white paling, some evergreen oaks with moss hanging on them, a dovecote, a stable and one of the immense water butts (attached to almost every house – a sort of well above ground which looks like a tower at the sides of the house and is often decorated with a dome). I never took so long a walk in any country without seeing more. There is more to draw in the walk from Paddington to Shoreditch.

Coming home passed a negro girl – handsome face and well made, perhaps fourteen. I looked at her and she was so unusually grave that I noticed it to Dr. B. Presently she came after us and asked me if I would hire her. She said she was free and would do anything merely for a home. – Now this struck me as strange because there is no lack of work here and wages, so I said sit down and then I talked to her and it came out, all in a torrent of strong indignation – that she would not go home again, that her mother had beaten her (she showed me a place on her arm, the skin off, and other marks of violence). Her mother had turned her out and locked the door on her. It was a long story and I was very sorry for the girl, who evidently spoke the truth. I told her I could not take her to England which she begged of me to do. I thought over and made her think as well as she could over the best course, and having decided on that gave her my address, etc., and then left her in a better state of mind, I hope. Her mother was a free negro, and no doubt my friends will say this comes of giving freedom to the African.

Friday, 8 January. Called on Mrs. Brooks, a friend of our landlady's. Mrs. Brooks has made her fortune by teaching dancing, as many others have done here in this ball-loving city. She is half English and half French, very agreeable, and has the manners of a certain gracious English Countess with the sharpness of the Yankee added. Very soon of course, she introduced the subject of slavery (n.b. all slave owners are on the defensive and begin to defend themselves as if they stood at the bar, and so they do, the bar of intelligent opinion). She told me slavery was suited to negroes, that masters rarely sold their slaves without giving them a choice in the matter. That she had bought her slave because the girl was tired of her mistress and wanted to come to her (Mrs. Brooks). She told me many stories of the affection between masters and servants, all of which I believe, and I believe slavery is only nominal in many cases of domestic slavery. She insisted that the *property* the whites have in their servants makes them much more kind then they would be if they only hired them. 'We feel towards them as toward our children.'

While I was with her Dr. B. was with three brothers from Algiers, two M.D.'s and other apothecary friends of his from Africa. He saw their names in the paper and went to see them.[49] They were enchanted to see him and told him this was the place for a M.D.; they are all succeeding well. They told him the best and cleverest people here were the quadroons. The quadroon doctors are famous. The quadroons are not admitted into any white society.[50]

Saturday, 9 January.   I think I told you that next door but one lived the family of a white man[51] by a black woman which, I have determined ever since I came, to make their acquaintance. Mrs. S. knows them on *business* relations, but refused to introduce me because she could hold no social intercourse with them. I boldly sent to the house and asked leave if I might draw their goat? They were very happy, so I went in this afternoon and made sketches and talked to the eldest daughter, a white girl with blue eyes. She was embarrassed at first, but after a little quite at ease and asked me to give her lessons in drawing. I shall, as she interests me much and she is rich and cannot better employ her money, I am sure.

The house was well furnished: music, pictures, books, etc. in the sitting rooms; dogs, cats, chickens, pigeons, a mockingbird, etc. in the yard. An amusing house and I will go in very often. They live quite a lonely life. Madame——was at the plantation with her husband. He has no white wife.

9th.   Dear Pater,

As it is nine days I expect our money today, so save my letters. Here it is £40! Good Mill[52] has sent it by telegraph so we are all right!!

We mean to stay here in this house making excursions to the Gulf, etc. for a day or two and returning to our boxes, etc. here until £100 comes. One of our French doctor friends has come in – so enchanted to see the Doctor. He is like Nanny and me. He says he cannot live without going back to Algiers. The idea of that lovely country is always with him. He is telling the Doctor if he would but stay a year here how much money he might get, etc., etc., etc.

Good night. All well and jolly. I shall be glad to get to Savannah. I long to see a view.

Your affect. Barbara.

Sunday, 10 January.
New Orleans.

Poor Mrs. Sillery! I have a long story to tell about her but my friend the Professor says it will excite no interest in England whatever.

You know that my Doctor doctored Mr. Sillery the ruined Englishman, and we both felt great interest in him because he is very clever and has invented a sewing machine which I think beats Grover and Baker's – simpler and as efficient. Mr. Sillery was condemned by the doctors here as consumptive and to die in two months. My doctor examined his lungs very carefully and pronounced him free from any lung disease but ill of that American disease of the nerves and stomach so common here. He took great pains to put him into a new track of life and told him above all he *must* leave off the morphine which these doctors had given him. Now that Sunday I went out with Mr. Sillery. I found out that Mr. Sillery was often delirious from taking too much, and the other night the whole house was roused by his ill treatment of his wife. He was mad or wicked or both, beat her, and threatened her with a loaded pistol, but she would not let anyone come into the room.

Next day Colonel of Police was burning to take him up. Mrs. Sillery was so afraid of her husband, though (she would not consent to his being taken up), that she lay hid all day in the back kitchen, shaking with fear. Of course I told her she was a fool and if she submitted to be beaten she did a greater wickedness than if she beat her husband: 'We have no right to let people be wicked – and you know you can get a divorce – You have two lawful causes: you support your husband, he does not support you, and he ill-treats you.' No use talking. What do you think she does instead of listening to my advice?

– why, goes to Madame Alventine, the 'only lady magician,' to get her fortune told and comes back and tells me all about it!

As I see three ladies advertise as magicians and astrologers there must be a good many people like my friend, and I consider her story as very illustrative of Southern life.[53]

Mr. Sillery thinks he has a right to his wife's earnings and is not satisfied though she gives him half, and every now and then bursts out into these dangerous furies. Dr. B. tells her he won't die. There is no hope for that release for her – he is not a man to die. He has the American nervous fever. It is curious to see how American Englishmen become in a few years here, quite as American as Americans.

The other day sailing down Prytania St.[54] with Mrs. Sherbourn I saw in the midst of the Brighton bathing-machines stranded there, one bigger, broader, expanding nearly over the whole of its little garden, and over the door was written 'Church of ——' (I should have said 'Church of the Mother of Bathing Machines'), but it was 'Church of the DIVINE HUMANITY.'

Today I was moved to go and see what the divine humaity was like, and went into the little house and found myself in a room filled with fifty chairs and twenty-two people and a pale preacher who said, – 'This is a spiritual church, etc. Perfect liberty dwells here, etc. Live by the spirit only – its incoming can be felt like electricity even in the natural man, etc. The more knowledge we get of the Divine Order the freer we become, etc. We have now internal seers, etc. Interiority, etc. Mediatorialship, etc. There are our divine revelations. There are three men in the one human: first the inner (the celestial, etc.), second the middle (the spiritual, etc.), third the outer (or natural, etc.).' After the sermon I spoke to him and asked him how he came by special revelations. He said, 'Come and converse with me next Tuesday.' 'Say Monday,' said his wife. 'No, Monday I am engaged,' said BLS. 'Ah, I was prompted by the spirit to say Tuesday – you see how even in the smallest affairs I am guided.' 'Good Morning, Sir.'

Tuesday, 12 January.[55] Evening, Dr. and I went, and having learned that Mr. Christy was an honest man (a lawyer who

82

preached for nothing but to diffuse his ideas), we went with more pleasure. He went off into a sort of trance and talked about *my* spirit (I asked him to tell me how he came by the gift of prophecy) and said a great many curious things, very Swedenborgian,[56] but ended by saying he was puzzled by the many spheres my spirit visited, etc., etc. So we came away as wise as we went and very tired.

Doctor is going to call on Dr. Nott. I expect they won't agree. The Doctor's ideas of Universal Fusion and Universal Brotherhood to spring from it are not popular here at all, though they can't deny the mulatto race here beats the white in health (see no. 1),[57] strength and beauty, and all the men admire the women with some African blood in them more than they do the whites. And I do not wonder, – the whites here are wretched looking objects, yellow and pale, the quadroons magnificent women, the mulattoes very often beautifully formed and faces of a sort of Memnon cast, very pleasing, the children of mixed unions exquisite little creatures, the white children little miseries.

At five o'clock went into the Black Church. There were eight hundred or a thousand negroes, slave and free, a white man preaching a wicked sermon about Judgment Day describing the tortures of the damned and I am sure he did not believe a word of it. The negroes shrieked and howled and repeated words, 'Be damned,' 'All be judged!' 'Justice done,' 'Blessed Lamb,' 'God my Lord,' jumping up and howling them out, and some of the women going on jumping and calling out until they fell down exhausted at the bottom of the pews. I do not wonder! If anyone sincerely believed in what the preacher said, he or she would go into convulsions and many of these poor people did believe and had imagination vivid enough to think of lost ones, perhaps dear ones, suffering such tortures because they had not joined the church.

After the sermon four babies and four or five adults were baptised. Two of the babies were very white, two mulattoes. One baby was as white as any white baby I ever saw – blue eyes and flaxen hair. Then we all sang 'Passing away,' and I went out and the Sunday School began. I wished much to stay but was quite tired from the excitement. I shall go again some Sunday.

I saw some noble heads there – two mulatto men with heads like a bust I remember, marked Vespasian, in the Vatican. They must have been brothers though they were not together. Many heads were like monkeys but the majority were not disagreeable in feature and had an attentive expression very touching to see.

A white lady spoke to me and said that she thought there was more religion among the African than the American race, that the poor suffering creatures turned naturally to their heavenly Father. I thought of a line of Mrs. Browning's: 'And they said God be merciful, Who ne'er said God be praised.'[58]

Monday, 11 January. In the evening went to the Lyceum[59] with Mrs. Brooks to hear a lecture – we did not know on what until the lecturer, Dr. Nott, got up and said *On the Immutability of Human Types*, and I remembered this very man had sent his books[60] on races to Algiers to Dr. Bodichon, having read his papers on races and the necessity of mixture of races! Curious coincidences.

Dr. Nott proved that races were distinct by referring to Egyptian tombs and showing the drawings of negro, arab, jew, asiatic, mongol, etc., and went on to say that climate and education could not alter races, and ended by saying he hoped that he had proved that certain plans of certain philanthropists to alter certain races were absurd: that as long as negro was negro they would be inferior to white ('Hear! Hear!') and must hold their present position ('Hear! Hear!'). The President thanked the lecturer; said as no one disputed or discussed he would read to them two paragraphs from the *Statistical Journal* of London which would show them the money argument was telling (a sneer) with the English – they were coming to their senses! The paragraph states the proportion which the cultivation of cotton bears to the whole amount of Southern industry, and the proportion the manufacture of cotton bears to the industry of England, and goes on to say the 'deductions concerning slavery from these statements are not necessary to draw here,' or words to that effect. 'Hear! Hear! Hear!' How I did burn to ask a few questions. It is not true races have been mixing ever since Pharaoh's time? How many pure negroes have you here like that type you show us? Do you apply this argument of slavery you build up from the African pure to all – even those who are more white than black?

After the lecture we looked at the curiosities and talked to some of the learned about rattlesnakes – a live one was in the room and made a horrid noise.

[*Thursday, 14 January.*[61]] . . . little inclined to walk.

She is deeply interested in Charlotte Brontë. I found the *Life*[62] on the table and the *Pictorial History of England*. She told me that England was her country, that she loved England and hated this place – though she has never been out of Louisiana.

Now I will, if I can, get this girl to come to Mrs. Reid's Home and College.[63] I think of it very often. How happy she would be! I suppose the mother and her children are free, but it is not at all certain. Very often the children of these unions are sold even after they have lived in luxury!

Friday, 15 January.   Nothing to say but of the weather which is detestable, better now than it was, for it lightnings and rain pours down. Last night it was stifling hot, this morning the air so heavy that I could not stay in the house. We should have been on the road to Texas if it had been fine. We want to see a bit of that railway.

We were out in a real hurricane. If the Dr. had not caught hold of me I should have been thrown into one of the filthy streams. I never saw so sudden a storm. The mud of the street was taken up and hurled in the air. I was quite covered with dirt.

Saturday, 16 January.   I see in the newspapers today 'Young Tornado'[64] and find ten or twelve people were killed by that *tourbillon* and an immensity of mischief done to the shipping and houses.

The air today is perfectly delicious – cool, fresh and pure, the sun brilliant. We went this afternoon over to *Algiers* (as the other side of the river is called),[65] and walked along the levee but nothing could we see but *terre plat* everlastingly and water, water, everywhere. What an insult to call it Algiers! We had some pleasant conversations with French and German work people who all seemed very well satisfied, excepting one old woman who longed to see her own Wirthenburg before she died, with her whole heart, and insisted I was German. She said she did not like anything in America. We said as we came back that we would never go to see that Algiers again – miserable impostor.

The woman who has dressed Mrs. B[rooks]'s hair for years is the slave of one of her friends, and this is her history. Her mother was a full-blooded African slave of M—. She was married to another of his slaves and had a large family.

M—'s wife died and he took this black woman to be his wife and suckle his infant son, at the same time freeing all her children and promising her her freedom. She had a second family by M—, he always promising her and her second family their freedom. He was content, but unfortunately he died suddenly without leaving them free. The slave was a faithful woman and had devoted herself to the son – was indeed the only mother he knew. But when he was twenty-one he sold her and all his brothers and sisters, though he knew his father's intentions. He tried also to claim the first family. This was told as nothing outrageous and received with no exclamations excepting mine.

I hear many such stories here from those who uphold the system. Mrs. Brooks has slaves and thinks it a good institution! Mde. B.[66] had had three husbands: first, dead, second was divorced and went to the Mormons, third was blown up in a steamboat. This is characteristic of America. Every third woman I meet seems to have been divorced.

In the courts of Philadelphia in ten years about 2700 divorces have been granted. Suits of this nature are increasing in frequency. Next door to M^e.B. lives a widow whose means of subsistence consist of two small houses and a negress whom she sends out to dress hair. This negress has a family of children by a white man, but the widow owns them and of course will sell them, and the father does not think about buying them nor did it enter the heads of either M^e. B. or Mrs. S. to suggest it as humane in our converastion. No, they are property of the widow. This negress M^e. B. says is a good-for-nothing woman. Mᵉ. B.'s Amy (a slave) told her that this negress seized the widow and shook her because the widow called one of her children a good-for-nothing hussy! The negress seized her mistress and said 'You dare illtreat my children, when I go out in all weathers to get you your living and bring back all I earn to you!' This is considered outrageous!

It is almost impossible for you to conceive the utter depravity to all ideas of justice caused by slavery. I still think the whites suffer most by slavery spiritually and physically.

Thursday, 21 January. The last few days we have seen a few people but have seen nothing exceeding curious. Heard more stories like the above.

I am astonished more and more at the stupid extravagance of the women. Mrs. H.[67] (who gains her living by keeping a boarding house) has spent, she says, at least £60 on hair dyes in the last ten years. All the ladies, even little girls, wear white powder on their faces and many rouge. All wear silk dresses in the street and my carmelite[68] and grey linen dresses are so singular here that many ladies would refuse to walk with me. Fashion rules so absolutely that to wear a hat requires the courage of Vanaurburg, or rather George Fox.[69] Leather boots for ladies are considered monstrous. I never saw such utter astonishment as is depicted on the faces of the populace when I return from a sketching excursion. I do not like to come back alone so the Dr. always comes for me.

The people in the house would lend me any amount of flower garden bonnets if I would but go out in them. This is so like the Americans – they are generous and kind but will not let you go your own way in the world. My little plain bonnet and plaid ribbon is despised, all my wardrobe considered shabby and triste. I never saw people dress so much, and I must confess, too, with a certain taste which is caught from the French.

Sunday, 24 January. Went to the church for coloured people. In the courtyard I stopped a very dark man and asked him if there were many slaves in the congregation. He said nearly all were slaves. I went in and heard the same singing which I had heard before and was more than ever struck with the intense expression of devotion on many faces.

After the singing a coloured man from his pew prayed somewhat after this manner: 'Oh heavenly Father, we would ask you to come down and visit our hearts this evening, fill us with thy love – it is only thy spirit which can turn us to righteousness – let this time with thee be a holy time for, withdrawn from all worldly thoughts – let thy spirit, Oh God, *brew around, about and within us – steep us in thy holy love*, etc. etc. etc.' There is something more pathetic than words can describe in the earnest devotion of this African race. I am sure they do believe in God and a future life with a vividness of faith very rare among Europeans.

Olmsted does not believe they are really religious – he calls it superstition.[70] Now I call it religion because, though this faith has a mixture of superstition (whose has not?), they take patience and consolation from their belief in God's justice and love. Did I tell you what happened to Mr. Spring[71] when he came South and visited a slave owner who had a sick daughter? The slave owner said, 'Will you come and hear my negroes pray? One prays very well' Mr. S. assented and they went to the negro quarters, and the master said, 'Now, Uncle Dick, give us a *short* prayer.' Uncle Dick began, 'Oh God almighty, maker of heaven and earth, etc., we thank thee for thy goodness to us daily etc. etc. etc. We bless thy name etc. Pray that *thy daughter be restored to health*!' He forgot God, you see, and thought only of his master's presence. But I think I told this before. But having done nothing to write of, I am hard up to fill my letter.

While I was in the church I believe Mr. Sam Smith went up with a balloon on the backs of 2 ALLIGATORS 11 feet long![72] I knew he was to have gone up but I preferred the negroes to this attractive performance of my respected relative.

Monday, 25 January. I have been very anxious to see the schools for coloured children. *Everybody* said there were schools, though no government schools, and I imagined these were like our schools – half charity, half pay. With great difficulty I got the address of the principal school and today I started off to the French part of the town to find it. I hunted in vain until a little mulatto girl of fifteen or sixteen said, 'I will take you,' and so she did. As we went she told me in French (she spoke both French and English) that she was free. I said, 'What do you do for your living?' She said, 'No good,' in English. I never should have found the school for it is a private house, nothing to show it is a school. I rang at the great porte cochère, and on asking to see the school was shown upstairs by a French gentleman with a very unpleasant face into a large dreary room in which were some eighty or ninety girls. The room was very untidy and dirty. (The floor was very dirty and scattered over with bits of paper, orange peel and rubbish. I never visited such an ugly looking school in all my life). Nothing in the room agreeable to look at except some of the children's faces. Another French gentleman was sitting at a high desk and came down to me, and then a woman teacher came to speak to me. She was not a lady and looked and spoke like a woman with little sense and less heart. I learned from this disagreeable creature that the school was a speculation, that the education was equal to that given to white young ladies in private school (very likely), that professors taught history, geography, English and French (singing not taught, no object lessons or class lessons, all teaching on the private school system), that the fathers of the girls and boys were most of them white living with coloured women *placées* (these women are called; to *placer* is the expression which means to live with a coloured woman. No marriages between coloured people and whites are legal here, so that to *placer* is very common and not considered disreputable. These unions, I should think from what I hear, are equal in respectability to the marriages between white women and white men – or nearly so. The teacher said most of these girls would *placer*). Four dollars a month is the lowest charge and there are many extras.

There is no other school of any size at lower price except the Catholic schools. I could get no other information out of this woman. She was Irish, I found out, and perhaps some relation to John Mitchell who is lecturing here against the English in India,[73] for she seemed to have a hatred to the Saxon. She called up the whitest girls for me to look at. They were so white and had so little African blood in them that I should not have suspected it. Miss Spooner[74] looks much more like a coloured girl than four or five I saw there.

I asked for the highest, cleverest girls and *they were not the whitest nor the darkest but were unmistakable negroes*. Some of the girls were beautiful, but all had a listless look which was probably the fault of the school. The teacher begged the girls to keep order as a lady was present! (in vain). Most of the girls were Catholic and I saw a dusty crucifix over the master's desk.

Although I had told the master that I wished to see the school simply because I was interested in the education of the coloured, Monsieur —— did not believe me and came up and asked if I had an *élève* to recommend. I repeated again my motive on which Monsieur showed me out in a great hurry.

It is sad if this is the best school. Here is work for the Abolitionists. Let six good New England women come here and set up a good private school for two dollars a month. Where is the school Mrs. Stowe was to found? I do not see why schools should not be founded for free blacks by private people, and this would do immense good.[75] They seem to have very few if any opportunities of getting a good education. And I am sure nothing but the elevation of the blacks themselves will bring about a happy emancipation.

Tuesday, 26 January. The air of the town was so oppressive that I took rail and went to the Lake, which is like going out to sea. I was enchanted to see how the trees have come out into flower and leaf since I was there last. I found a beautiful white tuber rose, not quite like any I have seen before but by its scent, form and colour I think it is a tuber rose.

In the train I had the usual amount of drunken Germans and Irish. 'By Jesus I'm curst if I don't leave this Goddamned train,' is a specimen of the conversation which one is obliged to hear because there is only one class! I cannot tell you how sick it makes me to hear this continual swearing. Olmsted says German Americans always begin a conversation with 'By Christ, gents etc.' I wish it were not worse than that.[76]

The conductor of the railway told me he had seen an alligator four feet long this morning just in the place where I drew – of course I went after him and of course he was not there.

Tonight I was sitting writing (Doctor gone out for an hour) with a candle. The window shutter being open I heard, I thought, a noise against the glass – but would not attend; when Doctor came home I heard it again – a voice – so we went out. There was a drunken German in our garden who had been looking in at me probably. In no country have I seen so many drunken men, as here.

Thursday, 28 January. I wanted much to see one of the private institutions for young ladies, having an opinion that they are very bad here. Mrs. Sherbourn said she could take me to one of the principal, so this morning we took rail to Greenville[77] and walked up a pretty French trimmed garden to large white house shaded by immense evergreen oaks, draped in the grey moss which today looked beautiful waving in the wind against an intensely blue sky. We explained our reason for coming but the Madame was determined to show nothing. She told me she had forty-five girls of the principal families in Louisiana; that they were terribly ignorant when they came to her; that many girls of fourteen did not know the name of the great river and one could not tell the name of the country she lived in (one girl of seventeen came to her who had never heard of Washington); that their heads at twelve were full of beaux and dress. She said parents took very little trouble about their children's education, much less trouble than in France. Madame was a very unsatisfactory woman, though this is considered one of the best schools.

After this visit I went to one of the Common Schools in the town. There, as usual, met with cordial politeness. The boys were intelligent and bright, the master good-natured and clever. Very satisfactory visit. The girls were, as usual, repeating history of their victories over the British, and seemed to understand and like their lesson. I liked the teachers so much that I invited them to come and see me. All these schools want object lessons. There is too much routine, but they are good and improving.

Came home and found the Doctor had had five ladies to see him – some of his 'codfish aristocracy' which I laugh at, because my friends are solid units, rich and quiet or poor and enlightened and his are flare-up fashionables or political sufferers. We had Judge Spofford,[78] a very distinguished man, one other evening and he told us many interesting things. Dr. Mole, the Spanish friend of the Doctor's and the French doctor came in the evening and talked until eleven about the mulattoes, creoles etc. To sum up he said, 'Mulattoes are more intelligent and more healthy and handsome than the creoles' (the whites born here). He said he had boldly stated this, his opinion, in a large company of Americans and creoles, and was absolutely hooted at and was near having to fight to maintain his opinion. He said he would rather marry a quadroon than an American.

He said French, Spanish and Americans degenerate in this climate, that he was assured the mixed race must triumph here, that natural causes would put the power into their hands in some years. He says the mulattoes here are not so strong as the mulattoes of Africa, that their white fathers are not so strong physically. Blacks sell for higher price than mulattoes excepting some mulatto women. There are in New Orleans many more mulattoes than negroes, but on plantations many more negroes than mulattoes.

We talked about slavery under Spanish laws in Cuba and he said laws were much juster for slaves. A slave may buy himself, or if he is dissatisfied demand his sale to another master for the same price for which he was sold.

We talked about the American rashness and the number of accidents in carriage, rails, steamboats. He said there was nothing like it in any country he had visited and that no people were so careless of life. All the stories he told would fill a book.

Did I tell you I was going down to visit one of the most renowned sugar plantations in Louisiana, belonging to Isaac Osgood. The Osgoods are very rich people and very pleasant.[79] You will hear more of them by and by. We came here shabby in dress and moneyless, and yet we have been treated like princes by all, high and low. Hospitality offered from everyone – total strangers who never heard of us and did not know even that I was cousin to Florence Nightingale[80] (I do not know who said I was, but at Cincinnati I found that added a brilliancy to my reputation – astonishing. I was told to say so by D— to insure a warm reception, but I refused positively).

Sunday, 31 January.
New Orleans.

The other day I went to return the visit of the D'Arcys, Dr. B.'s rich friends. They live in a country villa surrounded by a garden of roses and orange trees.

I found the young ladies (after the French fashion which prevails here) in their dressing gowns. There came in two ladies to call, dressed out in the most magnificent style – in brocade dresses, white kid gloves, etc. I sat still and heard the conversation: first, the clergymen were discussed, then the ball of last night, then a young friend lately married and it was hoped another young friend who was going to do the same would be more fortunate because the husband was very dissipated – 'if he were drunk at night we would say nothing about it, but to be drunk in the morning! – in the street! – in business hours! x x x he is a cotton marker and the young man who will marry her[81] – is a cotton weigher').

After this visit was over I asked Mrs. D'Arcy to tell me about the unhealthy season ('53) and she told me how she had nursed the sick and how the Howard Society[82] of ladies and gentlemen had exerted themselves turning schools into hospitals and taking turns going in bands to nurse the sick. She described their devotion and efficiency as wonderful. After the fever had abated they had nine hundred destitute orphans left on their hands. Their call for subscriptions was immediately responded to and they founded a home for the nine hundred little ones. She said these poor children had been left in the panic so uncared for that all their hair had to be cut off, and it was to her the most distressing sight to see the poor things staring in horror at one another, not used to the close shave. She took a wheelbarrow full of toys to try and make them play, but nothing could enliven them until their hair began to grow.

In spite of the Doctor's saying they were '*comme les gens de mon pays*,' I began with contempt for these people but I ended with hearty respect, and took their *brandy and water* when offered as if I drank it at every call I ever made. They are good people.

On Friday night I went to a concert.[83] On Saturday (30) to dinner with the Osgoods. They have near two hundred slaves and *sixty babies* in their nursery. It was a very pleasant family dinner. Dr. B. came for me at five – these Southerners have the absurd fashion of dining at three, so I cannot dine out without cutting up my day. I went to the Opera in the evening.[84] I have had two days of people-seeing because the weather is cold and I can't draw out or go into the country, and also because I was disgusted with my drawings.

Mr. Osgood thinks the moral state of America is worse than twenty years ago, this degeneracy caused by the influx of low Germans and Irish. Certainly America may take the motto of *Rubbish shot here*,[85] and certain it is also that this rubbish fills a vast hole on which will be built the greatest noblest edifice of a free nation! such as the world has never seen.

It is very instructive living in the house with the Chief of Police, and now I am a little used to his language. I like the man. He is very clever in his business, and we rejoiced with him yesterday when in the back of an oyster stall he found a hundred thousand dollars stolen two years ago![86] He nabbed the thief in a clever way. And think of it, the poor man robbed had taken to drinking, and when his money was given him died – a few hours afterwards!

You all know I am fond of seeing life and lots of life I do see! I wish I could send it all over to you it is so curious – horrible and so amusing.

I only grieve I cannot get acquainted *intimately* with one negro, all this time. No one can imagine the difficulty.

I have been to see one of the female M.D.'s here (there are two) Dr. Ely Cohen from the Pennsylvania College, a pleasant quiet woman who is getting practice here.[87] I liked her well enough to ask her to tea tomorrow.

She had read an account of me in a Philadelphia newspaper, how I studied nature in Europe, Africa, etc. etc. etc. etc.

Wednesday, 3 February. Dined at O[sgood]s. Had a long talk about free negroes. Mr. O. thinks they work well for wages. He had a footman who was a slave and then freed, and

94

he did his work just as well for wages as in slavery – not any better.

He says the greater part of the mulatto population of the town is free and a very respectable class, probably much better than the Irish. They consider the Irish much below them, but the social standing of the Irish is higher – they have votes and the right to go to the schools. He says some of the coloured people are excellent mechanics and some are learned and quite distinguished. He knows of one judge, one professor and some few others very remarkable. Many of the free coloured people are very poor and efforts have been made lately to employ them in factories, many are working at the sewing machines making clothes for the negroes.

He says free negroes will work for wages. In Barbados he says all the land is in cultivation and the negroes must work or starve, and they do work and the masters have less trouble with them than they did when they were slaves. In Jamaica there is land still wild where the negroes can live without work and they prefer that, but when they must work they do work. 'They are really religious,' Mrs. L[awrence] said, 'more truly so than the Irish.'

Mrs. O. said this town has much changed for the worse in forty years. When it was all French it was orderly and sober; now it is disorderly and the most drunken place on the earth.

But the Irish and Germans improve after they have been here some time. Mr. O. agrees with the Dr. in thinking when the vine is cultivated and wine is cheap that the people will be much improved in sobriety and par consequence higher in morality. The cheap whiskey ruins the people.

About snakes he told me that a few years ago when the levee gave way and the upper part of the city was flooded, that the snakes took possession of the houses and drove the inhabitants out. This also Mr. Hovat told us, and since we have been here a poisonous water snake was found close by our street.

While I was talking to Mr. O. a young tornado began to blow and the rain to fall in a torrent. These storms are not common so far up, but on the coast are of frequent occurrence and do great mischief. Mrs. L. said that the island where she and her children had been as a summer watering place had been absolutely submerged in one of these storms – not one house left and many hundred people drowned.

I hope, Pater, you have Olmsted's book *Our Slave States*; it is the best book I have seen on the Slave States. I feel that it has said nearly all I should say. Read Louisiana, page 631. I have heard such conversations.[88]

There goes the gun – the eight o'clock gun to send in the negroes. No one can be out now without a pass or, if he is, the watchman nabs him and sends him to jail right away.[89]

Did I tell you that I went with Mrs. Sherbourn to one of the astrologers (there are three near us)? I only waited in the outer room to see the people while Mrs. S. went in and asked if she might take lessons in the art! There were nine or ten ladies coming and going while I was there. I begin to think there are few ladies here who have not consulted some of these people. The old Africans are supposed to be especially gifted in magic, and they practice the same conjurations here that they do in Algiers, and many believe in the Great Serpent[90] even when professing Christianity.

As soon as the weather is fine I go down to the plantation. I like the O[sgood]s very much. They are very hospitable, like the rest of the Southerners, and unlike the rest simple and easy in their way of life.

New Orleans.
Wednesday, 10 February.

My dear Pater,

We have stayed here a week for nothing – that is, the visit to the plantation has come to nothing. The Lawrences' children are ill and this cold air is considered too severe for them out of town, so the family stays in New Orleans and I do not see the plantation which I am very sorry for, as it is one of the finest sugar plantations in Louisiana and I should have seen a new phase of negro life which would have been a good letter for you.

The letter I sent about last Sunday's adventures is the best letter I have written because I never was so interested in anything as that 'congregation.'

This week the air has been chilly but healthy and the skies cloudy and beautiful. I have only painted indoors and have walked about studying life in various forms here in the town. I went to see a refuge and school the government has established for girls found idling about the streets, orphans or girls with bad parents. It is a well-managed place and the matron well-chosen. Sometimes there are sixty, sometimes only sixteen – the greater part are Irish, of course. It was the Chief of the Police who took us there,[91] and he showed us as we went a street called Battle Row because the Irish are always fighting and murdering one another there. Four years ago two Irishmen murdered five others for an old grudge about Irish politics. In the Workhouse (which is a prison for small offences as well as a refuge for destitutes) I saw again Irish, Irish, most of them in for drink.[92]

The men work at their trades and one year (last year, I think) paid the expenses of the prison and eight hundred dollars over. I was astonished at the few precautions taken to keep the rascals in. When I was there, there were above two hundred prisoners in the place wandering about the vast court at their different trades and *only one watchman* and he went about with me as showman. He said they often did escape by putting the long planks used in the carpenter's room against the wall and running up. I wonder they did not all escape. I could not make the man say how many, but I suspect he did not care how many.

It is curious to see everywhere the want of officials. In Europe there are too many, in America every man is his own official, and in this prison every man was his own gaoler, I think.

The other night I spent with some free coloured people and had a most interesting conversation about slavery. Generally the conversation begins as this did, by, 'Have you read *Uncle Tom*?' then, 'It is called exaggerated,' then (as last night) I say, 'I suppose you know no cases like Legree's cruelty.' 'Oh, but we do, quite as bad.' And last night the lady told me that next door to her this very week the mistress had run a fork into the palm of the hand of one of her slaves and there it had stuck until it was drawn out. This mistress is very cruel – she is a German Jew. French, Germans, Irish are considered more cruel than creoles. Free blacks are also cruel sometimes. The worst case Mrs. V— knew was that M. Suzet of Natchez[93] who had more than a thousand slaves and exercised cruelties upon them too dreadful to tell, and yet was allowed to go on until he died. – Do you wonder if negroes think hell-fire is a necessity as God is a just God?

Mon. Dufan (friend of Dr. B.'s) knows a planter who, when he wants to make a slave confess, tortures him by having his teeth pulled out. This planter is alive and flourishing. I heard a planter last night (known to Mrs. Sillery) abused as very cruel because he allowed only one pound and a half of meat to his slaves daily and never had a doctor for them when ill.

Mrs. V. told me that Mr. H. (a planter she knows) would give all his four hundred slaves their freedom if he knew what to do with them, but they could not stay here. Liberia is a failure[94] and in the North they would be too harshly treated, so he stays on his plantation although he has very strong reasons for going to England or France. He has a family whom he acknowledges, by a woman of colour, and these children cannot get any education here except of the worst description and are excluded from all society unless it is the *placée* quadroon which he does not wish them to enter.

Mrs. V. I told you is a woman of colour, a creole of Louisiana. Now you know no free person of colour has a right to live here unless born here, and she was supposed by the police not to be of this state and served with a warrant, taken before the Mayor and had all the bother of proving herself a creole. You see the power of bother the police have. Every year the regulations concerning free negroes are more annoying. No sailors or cooks, etc. (if free coloured people) can land from the vessels unless by a pass from the Mayor and security from the Captain. No freed negroes can stay in the state unless born here and no free coloured people can enter, so that the free coloured population can only increase by births. I enclose a letter from Virginia which shows you the tendency of things and the fears of the owners.[95] It is a most unnatural state of things! I never was in a country where law interfered so wickedly with right. And I never was in a country where law was so little administered as here. I have given you a few instances; many others come before us which I do not write because there is often some hitch in the stories. Mrs. V. told me not to tell the Chief of Police that I visited her! or that I went to black churches. I know very well to call on a coloured lady is an unpardonable offence against the social code, but not against any legal code.

The Doctor sends his very kind regards to my father, brother and sisters, and Aunty and Mr. Gratton. Yr. affect. Bar.

Thursday, 11 February. I have read tonight nearly all of Miss Murray's book which has any opinions or facts about slavery. Lately also I have read Miss Bremer, and not long ago Stirling, Sir C. Lyell, and Dickens' notes[96] – and all seem to me to be very poor books on a rich subject. The two ladies lived with ladies and polite gentlemen and saw nothing of the life of the lowly I have seen during my nine weeks in New Orleans – a hundred times more of the real facts of slavery than those two ladies – and yet I could not dare to give my opinions except to say their opinions are founded on very insufficient data and that the evils I see here are immense, and the corrupting influence of this system so bad, so deep, that it seems almost impossible to exaggerate it.

To know the real character of the African you must not see him or her in rich families where you are a guest because they will always say just what the masters or mistresses like. Miss M[urray]'s experience of New Orleans is utterly insignificant and unworthy of attention; read Olmsted's if you wish to know something of the truth. He saw a great deal though he never seems to have become intimately acquainted with any negro or coloured person. I am happy to say that I am now quite at home in the house of Mrs. Moss (the illegitimate wife of a rich planter), and her three daughters and I are quite friendly. The eldest is more than friendly with me, quite affectionate. I have said little about them because I have come so suddenly into their secrets that I felt uncertain about many things concerning them. Now I understand them, but shall not give you their history as I hope you will see them some day. My acquaintance with them has shown me much of African and New Orleans life which no English lady ever saw before.

This morning Mrs. Dr. Cohen came to take me to Franklin School for one of the Public School Examinations. She has a daughter there. I was amused as we walked down at her telling me she wished so much to give her little girl (nine years) a taste for anatomy – but the child hated it and loved the outside of things – forms, colours, all trifly things, better than anatomy! Nature is stronger than mothers. These Women's Rights women are all on the same tack, longing to make facsimiles of themselves. I tell them all they are wrong and absurd – have the children to grow up as they will, to be cooks and milliners, soldiers or sailors if they wish it. The school examination was very unsatisfactory and stupid so I came away. Miss Carmichael's would have done better.

When it was dusk I went in to see Mrs. Moss because Anna M. is ill (I go very often there). I told her where I had been in the morning, whereupon she stormily, bitterly expressed her opinion that the schools were bragged up, but that the girls learnt nothing but to call folks 'dirty niggers.' That they do call all coloured people 'dirty niggers' is true, but Mrs. B. the principal does not teach it.

Mrs. Moss and her three daughters were arranging their library – several hundred volumes. I helped for a few minutes and not finding Miss Murray, I asked for it. 'What? you have not read that bad book!' 'No, why bad?' 'I tell you, it is an infamous book.' But why I could not get out of Mrs. M.

Miss Murray is supposed here to have been sent out by the Queen to report to her on the South! I was told she herself said so. This I do not believe but it was the impression when she was here and accounts for some things she saw!

Friday, 12 February. Early this morning I had occasion to call on a lady of colour who has four slaves in the house. I saw at a glance that she had been striking a little boy of nine who waits at table. His cheeks were red as fire, his skin is not too dark to show the red marks of slaps. Mrs. St. B. told me she had been scolding all the morning and had sent out for some leather straps to flog one of the women. Another day she said she had beaten a girl twice before I came in. She said she preferred to flog her servants herself to sending them to the Workhouse which most ladies did. She thought that a cruel proceeding, and said she only did it once when a girl ran away and was tied on a ladder the usual way and ordered twenty-five lashes, but they were so severe that Mrs. St. B. thought she would not live if all were given.

Now the flogging is done at the Parish Prison, not at the Workhouse.[97] Every day there are many whipped. It is one of the sights here but I can't stand quietly and look at such things. The accounts in books are enough. You must not imagine Mrs. St. B. is cruel – very far from it – but she is violent, and has to do with human creatures who have had no 'bringing up' and whom she expects to make fit into *civilized* life!

As far as I can see her four servants are not worse than certain animals Mary Carpenter[98] knows, and their bringing-up about equal.

Mrs. St. B. told me how greedy for money all negroes were. She said on two plantations she knows a prize of fifty dollars was offered to the best picker of cotton. The negroes worked so hard that the masters were afraid that they would injure themselves and so gave the prize to the one who was ahead and divided twenty-five dollars among the rest.

There are many very clever free coloured people in the town, she says, and I know it is true.

It is positive nonsense to talk of the rarity of buying and selling, or the separation of children and parents as uncommon!

A lady yesterday told me her brother (a minister in Georgia and a slave owner), as soon as a negro girl is fifteen, takes her out into the field and says, 'Now you must look about and choose a husband and when you have found one who likes you come to me and you shall be married.' He believes that if the girls choose they have more children than if they are chosen. The lady who told me this does not think slavery a very bad thing. The ladies were very fashionable – but not very intelligent. The youngest lady told me she was a very acute observer! and had seen New Orleans in a few weeks. Her father has a sugar plantation but she and her mother live in New York, as so many planters' families do. She was like almost all the young ladies I see in America, yellow, skinny and sickly, but with good features and oval face. The gentlemen talked of a case just decided (today, I understood) – I may make some slight mistakes but the facts are correct. Mr. M—.

had a large family by a slave woman and, being ill, made his will (in *1855*) leaving his children their freedom, and if the laws of the state would not allow them to be freed leaving them to the executors to receive their freedom in some state where they could be freed. In *1857* a law was passed preventing emancipation,[99] but few people entertained a doubt but that these slaves could be freed. The executors delaying to give them freedom, they (the slave children) appealed to law and the decision of the highest courts was *that they could not be freed*. I state for the credit of the gentlemen that they spoke of it as horrible.

I heard a great deal about the plantation – the solitude of the life down there and the misery of having no society excepting two or three hundred niggers!

Saturday, 13 February.   Mrs. P. (the wife of a sugar planter) came to call on me. She is creole but her parents are *of the North*. I have seen no one here towards whom I have felt so much sympathy and esteem as towards her. She looks like one of the old Puritan stock. Today for the first time we had a little confidential talk about 'the institution.' She told me that one of her relations who owned a plantation wished to free all his negroes gradually – would have freed them at once if he had thought it right, but she said, 'Freed negroes cannot live in Louisiana – the Northern states will not receive them – and sending them to Liberia is cruel. Mr. —— whom we know has received letters from his negroes there, and many are absolutely starving – that plan is a failure.

'My relation hoped to prepare the way gradually for the amelioration of his people and their ultimate freedom. But it is very difficult to know what to do.'

She told me on their estate the negroes were so very happy that she did not think any would leave there except perhaps some hands lately bought. She has a church and all the negroes are compelled to go once on Sunday; if not, there are many who would not go, she says. Some years ago they had many Congos – now only one remains and he clings to his old idolatry in spite of all she can do to cure him of it. She dare not instruct the mass of the negroes because it is contrary to law, but she teaches every one she can to read and to write who come near enough to her! She loves the plantation and tries to do all the good she can there.

Mrs. P. took me to see a picture which produces a great sensation in America wherever it is exhibited: Peale's *Court of Death*, an immense allegorical picture with twenty-three figures as large as life.[100] It is very badly painted, the figures ill-drawn and inelegant, which as the picture is on the Greek model is unpardonable. The allegory is not perfect: the *ministers* (war, famine, apoplexy, consumption, suicide, etc.) have men about to die mixed up with them. This spoils the picture, for the picture has the merit of being interesting and the monarch (stern and calm sitting in the cave heavily clothed in sable drapery, the head and shoulders almost lost in shadow) is a fine idea for the King – but badly done. There is very little knowledge of art in America, very little love of any art, but scarcely any for landscape art or small treasures like old Hunts.[101]

Some people like my drawings because they see they are like their woods but only one person has *enjoyed* them here, and that was a poor Italian image boy[102] who came two or three times and looked at me painting for a long time through the window and enjoyed the colours, he said. When he went away the last time he begged of me to accept a bas relief of some horses, young and old together, which he said I might paint into a field with trees round them.

As all my paintings are finished and my easel packed up I seem to have unlimited hours in the day, so I went to a Slave Auction. I went alone (a quarter of an hour before the time) and asked the auctioneer to allow me to see everything. He was very smiling and polite, took me upstairs, showed me all the articles for sale – about thirty women and twenty men, twelve or fourteen babies. He took me round and told me what they could do: 'She can cook and iron, has worked also in the field,' etc., 'This one a No. 1 cook and ironer –,' etc. He introduced me to the owner who wanted to sell them (being in debt) and he did not tell the owner what I had told him (that I was English and only came from curiosity), so the owner took a great deal of pains to make me admire a dull-looking mulatress and said she was an excellent servant and could just suit me. At twelve we all descended into a dirty hall adjoining the street big enough to hold a thousand people. There were three sales going on at the same time, and the room was crowded with rough-looking men, smoking and spitting, bad-looking set – a mêlée of all nations. I pitied the slaves, for these were slave buyers.

The polite auctioneer had a steamboat to sell, so I went to listen to another who was selling a lot of women and children. A girl with two little children was on the block: 'Likely girl, Amy and her two children, good cook, healthy girl, Amy – what! only seven hundred dollars for the three? that is giving 'em away! 720! 730! 735! – 740! why, gentlemen, they are worth a thousand dollars – healthy family, good washer, house servant, etc. $750.' Just at this time the polite gentleman began in the same way: 'Finigal Sara, twenty-two years old, has had three children, healthy gal, fully guaranteed – sold for no fault, etc. and six hundred dollars? Why, gentlemen, I can't give you this likely gal,' etc. etc. Then a girl with a little baby got up and the same sort of harangue went on until eight hundred dollars, I think, was bid and a blackguard-looking gentleman came up, opened her mouth, examined her teeth, felt her all over and said she was dear or something to that effect.

I noticed one mulatto girl who looked very sad and embarrassed. She was going to have a child and seemed frightened and wretched. I was very sorry I could not get near to her to speak to her. The others were not sad at all. Perhaps they were glad of a change. Some looked round anxiously at the different bearded faces below them, but there was no great emotion visible.

I changed my place and went round to the corner where the women were standing before they had to mount the auction stage. There were two or three young women with babies, laughing and talking with the gentlemen who were round, in a quiet sad sort of way, not merrily. The negroes laugh very often when they are not merry. Quite in the corner was a little delicate negro woman with a boy as tall as herself. They were called on together, and the polite gentleman said that they were mother and son and their master would not let them be separated on any account. Bids not being good they came on down and I went up to them. The girl said she thought she was twenty-five and her son ten. She came from South Carolina. She had always lived in one family and her boy had been a pet in her master's house. He sold them for debt. He was sorry but he could not help it, and her young missises cried very much when they parted with her boy. She was religious and always went to church. She was much comforted to hear there were good black churches in this strange country. While we talked two or three men came up and questioned her particularly about her health; she confessed it was not strong. They spoke kindly to her but went about their examination exactly as a farmer would examine a cow. It is evident (as Mrs. P. said this morning) planters in general only consider the slaves as a means of gaining money. There is not that consideration for them which they pretend in drawing-room conversations. The slave-owners talk of them as the Patriarchs might have spoken of their families and call it a patriarchal institution always, but it is not so – they do not consider their feelings except in rare instances. They tell you in drawing rooms that marriage is encouraged. – It is a farce to say so, if the father is not considered as a part of the family in sales. Of course there are exceptions and my experience is very limited. I came away very sick with the noise and the sickening moral and physical atmosphere.

Before I went the young man in our house had said, 'Well, I don't think there is anything to see – they sell them just like so many rocking chairs. There's no difference.' And that is the truest word that can be said about the affair. When I see how Miss Murray speaks of sales and separations as regretted by the owners and as disagreeable (that is her tone if not her words), I feel inclined to condemn her to attend all the sales held in New Orleans in two months.[103] How many that would be you may guess, as three were going on the morning I went down.

Sunday, 14 February.
New Orleans.

I went down to my Baptist friends at half past ten and finding only one old negress there sitting under the veranda I was afraid there would be no church but she asssured me there would be in time, that she came early, that church would begin at twelve o'clock. So I sat down and there came straggling in other old ladies and gay young ladies and fine gentlemen in spotless shirts and broadcloth of various complexions from pale yellow or olive to jet black or rather *deep chocolate with blue lights on it*, which is the blackest complexion I have seen here.

We all shook hands and sat and talked in the most friendly manner. They were very cheerful and pleasant. One old lady, nearly white, said she was very ill yesterday and thought her time was come, whereupon her friend said, 'Ah yes, what children we are. We fix ourselves all ready to go but God don't want us – we must abide his time and *he will tackle us up pretty quick*. He knows when it is right to fix us. Why, I remember being very ill and feeling sure I should die, so I gets out of bed and puts on a clean shift, washes my face, and unlocks my door and I lies down all decent and ready.' The old lady said she had been very ill and had administered the sacrament to herself, blessing the wine and bread, and after that she lay down and exclaimed, 'Lord, come. I am ready fixed, oh Lord.'

The handsomest dressed woman (and the woman whose face expressed the greatest intelligence) told me she was free. She had bought herself. She had a book in her hand and a Sunday School newspaper. She told me she attended the Sunday School of Christ Church, that there white ladies taught free coloured people. She was near fifty and was learning to read. She told me she was a washer and ironer and gained a good living, but that many free coloured women were not respectable. I wish I could give you every word of the conversation but I cannot do it. I have so much to write.

Presently came a mean-looking white man who wished to preach. He said he was sent by some other minister. The negroes were nervous but told him the Revnd. Benjamin was going to preach, when the polite old bully the police officer came up and said to the small white man (who was very like the Revnd. Kenrick, Pater's particular friend),[104] '*Sir!* no preaching here by anyone I don't know, Sir! Where do you come from? What is your name, Sir? I know nothing about you. You can't come here. The coloured folks have their own preacher.'

The little gentleman was frightened and went off. 'How do I know he is not one of your Northern men, one of your sneaking abolitionists, etc., and he asked me if I knew him. Then there came another white man who was allowed to preach there, so I would not stay. I know so well how they preach.

I went on to the Methodist and seeing a black man in the pulpit I went in and took my old place. He was in the midst of the history of the woman of Samaria and the congregation in a state of great enjoyment. 'Now Christ was going to Jerusalem and the city of Samaria was right in the road so he thought he could go there on his way, and my brothers you see he had a very little time to do anything so he wished to convince them he was a prophet as quick as possible, so he devises this plan.' (A good description of the difference between Jew and Samaritan came in here and moral charity). 'I like a well. I like a seat by a well. It is a pleasant place and Christ knew that women like to sit down and talk, so when he comes to this well he sees a woman and he asks her for water to drink. Now, my brother, Christ was not thirsty – it was only for conversation that he said, "Give me a cup of water." Now, my brother, this woman was not of the fairest character and Christ knew that, so he said to her, "Go call thy husband," and she said "I have no husband"' (the manner of giving this was so comical that all the negroes showed their white teeth and some laughed out loud). 'Then our Lord told her she had had five husbands! Now he knew very well that women like talking and that too he knew he could not do better than speak to a woman. He knew she would run and tell it all directly, and say, "Here is a prophet", and mark, my brothers, how she exaggerated as women will. She runs to the city and calls out, "A prophet is come who has told me everything that ever I did!" Now, my brothers and sisters, Christ had only said, *"You have had five husbands, and the last is not your husband,"* and you see how she thought that was everything. Perhaps it might be, my brothers, that her conscience suddenly waked up and she felt all her sins in the presence of Christ and that she felt as if he had told her all. x x x Christ did not care for *opinion religion*. All he wanted was *heartfelt* religion – be born again, be born again in the heart!' (Here was a shout of 'yes! oh yes, blessed Lord!' and jumping up and down with their hands up in the air – one day a man jumped himself quite out of his trousers.)

He spoke about the Jews and the captivity, and I remarked as I have often done that they (the congregation) always identify themselves with that chosen people in bondage and look forward to the release. Some look to heaven, but some, I am sure, look for a better time on earth.

They sang 'I'm going home to glor*ie*. Peter, John I then shall see. I'm going home to glor*ie*. Matthew, Luke I then shall see. I'm going home to glorie, etc.' I think they put in the names of anyone they wanted to see, for they sang different names – all the time stamping time, so that as the singing *surged* along I felt carried along too and sang with them. One old lady sang so intensely that she dropped down from exhaustion. There was no occasion to say to her (as all of the men called out to another old lady who was timid), 'Sing up, my sister, sing up!'

I spoke to some of my friends. They told me the prayer meeting had been 'beautiful.' How I wish I might get in, but I am a Gentile they say.

I dined with a coloured lady who was in the chapel, a planter up the river, such a shrewd, clever little old lady, rich and very hospitable. She told me that numbers of Italians, French and Irish come and ask her for a lodging. The other day a poor old Italian who looked very miserable slept at her house, and in the morning rang the bell and asked the servant to bring him a looking-glass to shave by – cool for a beggar. I like the little old lady and if I had time would go and see her plantation. Just off for Mobile.

Morning. Tuesday, 15 February.
Gulf of Mexico.

We are in a blue sea with a blue sky overhead and warm but fresh breeze blowing, not enough to toss us uncomfortably. Our good iron steamer *Virginia* is getting along well, so we shall be in at ten a.m. – we started yesterday at five o'clock. Fare is only $2, two meals and first-rate accommodations.

Last evening we sat an hour on the pier at the Lake Pontchartrain waiting for the boat, and by us sat a gentleman and lady from Illinois. The gentleman was very ill, travelling for health. Doctor said he had the smell of death and sure enough it was so, for after we had been on board for three hours he dropped down in faint and died. Doctor B. and another were with him but nothing could be done, he was gone in an instant! The poor wife was all alone – no servant, no one even knowing their names – but the ladies went to her and the gentlemen undertook all the rest – for in this climate attention to the dead must be given immediately. The gentleman was a Mason and on board there are Masons who will see to all for the poor lady at Mobile. She means to take the body to Illinois with her.

This sudden death you would have thought would cast a dark cloud over our ladies on board, but no, it is not so at all. I heard the kind lady who consoled the poor sobbing woman last night by telling her he was happy in heaven and that she herself had suffered in the same way – and had to keep up her courage, etc., laughing just as merrily the next half hour though they were dressing the body in the cabin. I do not think the Americans think so much of death as we do. I see the poor lady sitting in the cabin with the others this morning so I suppose their sympathy does her good. I hope it does.

My doctor has found a poor French working man (going to Mobile for work) ill of fever, whom he has been consoling and assisting and in return the Frenchman has told him part of his story. He was in the Crimea, he says (but the Doctor says *il ne faut pas croire* all that the French say), but one thing, whether true or not, I will give you. He says a French officer, hating England and wishing to insult the perfidious Albion, put his Victoria Medal round his dog's neck and would not take it off, upon which the French shot both dog and man.

There was a great deal of talk about Spiritualism in the cabin yesterday. One lady said she knew a lady whose husband put her into an asylum because she believed in the spirits, and that after being confined some time the physicians sent her out saying she was not mad, but the husband continued to persecute her. You can hardly imagine the bitter feeling that is growing up between believers and non-believers. I have seen the names of twenty-three newspapers devoted to spiritualism! How many more there may be I dare not say!

While I was at New Orleans there were two mediums from

Boston there. One, the editor of the *BANNER OF LIGHT*, gave lectures and sermons and showed pictures purporting to have been executed by spirits. I did not go to that, but I went to a private meeting at the house of some friends of friends of the Doctor's. There were eighteen or twenty believers and I thought it a waste of time, for they would not let me, a stranger, suggest any tests. The medium was a Bostonian and a cheat, a little tipsy I think, and a good ventriloquist, as he confessed himself.

The lawyer (minister of the Divine Humanity Church) is the best proof of faith in spiritualism. He is a young man and has married a grandmother by direction of spirits. That shows faith, don't it!

Dearest Aunt Julia,

Please send this to Pater or Nanny.

All well and jolly. We have had no letters for ages and shall not until we get to Savannah in six or seven days.

Dear Pater,

Hope you are all well and mark our journey on the map. Weather lovely.

yr. Bar.
Mobile, Alabama.

Roper House, Mobile.[105] We are in the pleasantest, quietest house we have been in since we left England. It is a second-rate inn, small like an English country inn. Weather lovely. Mobile looks rather pretty from the water, but all the country is as flat as (possibly flatter) than any flounder.

We are going out to post this and to make acquaintance with Mr. Neill's brother, Mr. Henry N., who lives here and to whom we have a warm introduction. We go on up the river in a steamer tomorrow evening and shall be at Montgomery in three days! Plenty of time to write on steamboats.

Wednesday, 17 February.
Mobile.

I like Mobile. It is a clean and cheerful town in a sandy soil, a great contrast to the mire on which New Orleans is built. Our friends in New Orleans said Mobile was just like New Orleans, but there is no comparison between the two places – Mobile is so much the more respectable looking and I am sure much healthier. Yesterday we walked out into the country. Quite delightful to walk on the solid earth after the mud of New Orleans. I cannot help thinking the Great River will some day take a turn there and walk across the country. I should not like to be there. What an awful rush of water it would be!

We are now out of New Orleans and can therefore abuse it. It is the dirtiest town without any exception that I ever saw. There seems to be no attempt at public cleanliness and private houses follow the public streets; there is no drainage system[106] and what dirty water runs from the houses is above ground, in sight. I only wonder they do not have fever every year there. Probably the constant rains prevent it. After the rains, I must confess, I never felt a more exquisite air than at New Orleans (if you are out of a stink).

Mobile has none of the foul filth of New Orleans. It is a very pleasant place. We walked into the county which is like Weybridge (but not so pretty). The fir trees are very fine and I found growing under them a little blue flower with four pointed petals – one of the sweetest little tiny flowers I ever saw in my life.

Today we drove farther into the country and went to the highest point in the neighbourhood, Spring Hill, the seat of a Military College.[107]

Mr. Henry Neill was very urgent for us to stay and see his family and friends, and Mrs. LeVert *the lady of the South*,[108] but we would not stay, being anxious for letters and another station for a month.

We are on board the *LeGrand* for Montgomery going up the beautiful Alabama.

Although the country round Mobile is much pleasanter and I like Mobile better than N.O., there is nothing so strangely fantastic and curious as the cypress swamps and probably I should not have had such interesting life as I had with my friends at N.O. At Mobile we should have been in the society of the place, and once in – no getting out.

I found in Mobile very good book shops. A bookseller told me that Ruskin's works sold well and Lewes's *Biographical*

Philosophy, etc., C. Brontë's life is everywhere.[109] Mixed with these books a few productions of the South such as *The Christian Doctrine of Slavery*,[110] etc.

This boat is crowded with a disreputable looking set of people. To one only (a blind woman) have I offered any attentions, but someone has paid me the disagreeable attention of going into my cabin and investigating the contents of my beloved black bag Aunt Julia gave me. My doctor, knowing I have all my painting things in it, carefully hid it under the pillow. This and its weight excited attention and some one bent the frame, put in a hand, undid my tin paint box, felt all the queer little damp pots and found nothing at all! Of course I told the clerk at once. He says it is very common!

Thursday, 18 February.
Alabama River.

This is a beautiful river! more beautiful than the Hudson, the Mississippi or *la belle Rivière*, the Ohio. The banks are a tangle of forest – deep, thick forest. Magnolia and firs are green and the rest are enveloped in the grey misty [? miry, ?wiry] drapery of moss. Last night just as the sun set (like a ball of fire in a blue and lilac mist, and the upper clouds were like changing colours in a pearl shell) we passed a tributary river, a deep quiet river coming through dense, thick forests – no boats, no birds – nothing stirring, not even a stag swimming across it. It was the most beautiful picture I have seen in America. In the still water was the lovely sky over again until we passed and made waves. All down into the far distance, one side green copper colour, the other side violet blue.

There was not one of the two hundred crew out to look at the sunset. I never saw a people so utterly without perception of the beautiful. I went into the cabin and looked round and saw a small boy five years old lying on the sofa, his legs stretched out over the cushions – when there were old people without seats. Yesterday at the *table d'hôte* at Mobile there were two little children *alone*, one not more than two, the other four. The littlest (for the other was little) could not reach the plate with her chin, yet she ordered without hesitation three different meats and tea with all the aplomb of a woman. The negress waiter asked the children what they would have just as if they were grown up! The children here are detestable. I do not say American children because it is very likely the most objectionable are Irish or German.

Last night the negro sailors danced while one played on the violin. It was the drollest sight in the world. They enjoyed it so intensely and moved with such extraordinary agility – so fast and then slow, now all on their heels then all on their toes. This was the first time I have seen them dance and I hope it won't be the last.

It is impossible to write or draw well on board these high-pressure boats. There is a constant shiver running through them. 'There's a mighty heap of danger,' says a woman here close by me, and 'a mighty heap of boats blown up.'

Friday, 19 February.
Montgomery.[111]

This evening we walked about this pleasant town. It is beautifully situated on seven or more hills clustering together, and on the highest is the Capitol, a fine building with a Dome. We went in and saw the House and the Senate chamber, and there lying on the top of reports of bills passed I saw Miss Dix's *Remarks on Prisons and Asylums.*[112]

I like this place. Everyone looks clean and well off, schools and churches bright and white as new pennies. Children polite and pleasant. Puppies divinely fat and grave (as I know, having made love to two today). One little black Newfoundland with waddling little legs and thoughtful blue eyes (which and his nose I wiped with my handkerchief, for he had a chronic cold) will make it painful for me to leave tomorrow at eight o'clock a.m. for Macon.

The Dr. says I want to bring home all America but it is only these few things:

A nigger preacher
A nigger infant schoolmaster
500 singing niggers
2 mulatresses
4 quadroon beauties
2 handsome mulattoes
2 puppies
1 raven

1 alligator
1 red bird
and 1 black babby for Aunt Julia.
Good night.

Yr. affect. Bar.
Montgomery,
Alabama
U.S.

February.   When I wrote from Montgomery I did not know what remarkable people we were (or rather were supposed to be), but I noticed that on board the *LeGrand* we received very particular attentions and that when the Dr. and I were sitting on the upper deck that every one of the gentlemen came up and, standing at a respectful distance, looked very intently at the Doctor – not rudely but with great curiosity.

At the Montgomery station a gentleman came up and talked to me and asked if my husband was not General Commonfort the Ex-President of Mexico[113] – he said it was reported so on board the boat. He told me the General had arrived at Mobile Tuesday, the same day we had arrived. He said General C. had been robbed of $2000. – This accounts for the attempt on my paint box: that bag was supposed to contain Mexican dollars.

Well, we laughed and got into the railway carriage. – Now I know you will think I am making up a story but it is not so. We have a certain affinity for adventure which exceeds and astonishes my imagination. You must know that the General is much respected here for the reform measures he tried to pass and which were the cause of his downfall.[114] No sooner were we seated than we remarked that all the occupants of the other carriages walked through ours and examined us, and when we stopped at a village the news spread and up came a crowd who gazed in at the windows *sans ceremonie.*

Now we began to appreciate the great advantages of being somebody in America! And to pity from our very souls all the Bremers, Dickens, Mackays, and Thackerays.[115] It seems to me it must be impossible to see anything in America if you are a distinguished person – all the ways of seeing are blocked up with eyes looking at you. Finding out I spoke English, the

PLATE 2

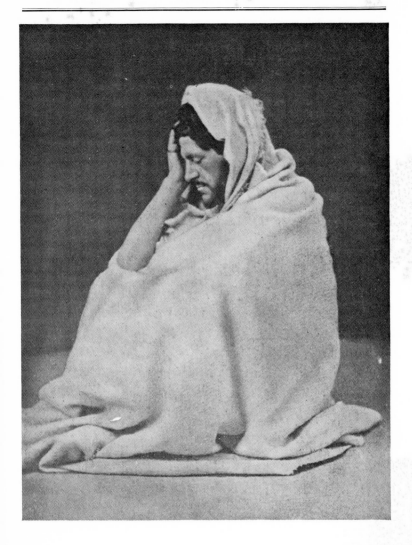

Eugène Bodichon

conductor came to me and after some polite speeches asked when we left Mexico. I told him it was all a mistake but I do not believe he believed a word I said, for the mistake continued in full force. Perhaps like a true American he went and told the rest that we were real Mexicans – that I said so.

At Columbus we had to wait in the town for an hour and most of the passengers went to the grand hotel. We preferred to wander about the town. Presently a negro waiter runs up to us with a polite message from the hotel – then we see knots of people collect as the rumour spreads – and we poor helpless creatures could do nothing to stay it – (do you remember in Virgil the description of rumour stalking over the land[116] – I thought of it and it made me laugh). Now a crowd of gentlemen collect and stand in a line as we pass. They find me very Spanish, particularly the hands and feet (– but you must picture me – little brown waterproof jacket and pockets, black silk shirt, very short leather boots – very Spanish?)

At last, red in the face and very much flurried, the Master of the hotel runs out and says 'Illustrious General, you can not hide yourself – we heard you were coming – you can't prevent the people from wishing to see you, distinguished General – will you not come into the ladies' saloon to escape the public gaze, etc.' Then I (dying with laughter) interrupted him, and told him it was all a mistake and we ourselves did not know in the least how it originated.

Report is not easily stopped. When we were in the train again I heard it again from mouth to mouth, 'Commonfort,' 'Commonfort.' One lady as I passed seized my dress and said, 'Where do you stop,' then she came and sat by me and said, 'Oh, how young you are,' in tones of intense pity for my misfortunes. 'What lovely little hands you have – You bear the journey better than the President!' (The doctor had rolled himself up in white burnous so that nothing was visible but an Arab-like hump.) Her manner was that of one determined to admire me as an Ex-Presidentess and *belle dame d'espagna* – the cool impertinence of it struck me very much, being only a working woman.

You can't imagine anything more curious than to hear all the remarks, for until I spoke English it was taken for granted we could not understand. 'What a noble Spanish head,' said some. 'Bless me! he don't look like a President.' 'Oh, that's their way of dressing.'

All day long this ghost of greatness haunted us, and even at night it was not laid though the Doctor wrote his name in full in the book. The son of the house showed us our rooms and said, 'There is a Mexican soldier in the house.'

The Doctor was amused to see a phase of American character new to us, but it was very fatiguing and we were glad enough our celebrity was for one day only.

> *Tuesday, 23 February.*
> *Savannah.*[117]

My dear Pater,

I hope you are all well, but no letters from home here for me.

I wrote to you or Nanny from New Orleans, Mobile and Montgomery in the last nine days, long letters which I tried to make as interesting as possible.

Love to all,
Yr. affect.

Barbara

It is so wet that I can't look round to see if there is work for me here for a month.

Evening of 23d. This curious mistake continues. All the ladies have been finding out beauties in me and talking until I was obliged to stop them. I happened to have on my green silk shirt, green net on my hair Ellen A. gave me, and to be writing with a green feather pen. This accidental picturesqueness was commented upon in the drollest manner! 'What a perfect picture, what taste these people have!' 'Bless me, what hair. How original to put it in a net!' etc. etc. I don't believe they believe me now! What are we to do! I am quite tired of being a Mexican Donna!

Doctor has just told me that in the reading room they spoke to him as General, and he denying the title they insist, and bring the morning's paper in which they point out:
'Distinguished ARRIVAL.
General Commonfort has taken up his abode at the Pulaski House. The General is accompanied by his daughter.'
Is it not too absurd!

In the train I read the Governor of Alabama's speech to the Legislature on its opening last November. I send you some extracts[118] because they are expressive exactly of the feeling I see everywhere, particularly with regard to the efforts to be made for the continuance of slavery institutions – by the education of the Southerners in their doctrines, etc. All the opinions expressed on other things seem to me remarkably sound – how distorted every view becomes where slavery is concerned, I leave you to judge. He speaks of the possibility of the severance of the Union, the necessity of warlike preparations.

All the Southern papers quote *The Times* as advocating a return to slavery! Is it true?

There is a strong and bitter feeling against the influence of the army of Northern teachers who fill the schools and great efforts are making to establish training schools for teachers in the Southern states. People talk of disunion very often and seem to think it very probable.

If the measure now before the Louisiana Legislature (to tax Massachusetts goods, etc.) (see B[119]) passes, it is war already between the states.

Stirling gives too favourable a view of the state of things I think. Not too favourable an account of the fat and merry look of the negroes – that would be impossible. They are physically better off, I believe, than the lowest classes in England or France.

My dear Pater,

I hope you are quite comfortable about me and will not wish me to come home until I have studied the New England States and sent you home a particular account of the state of things there.

We left Massachusetts to the last because we wished to have the best impression of America before leaving. It would be quite wrong to leave this wonderful world without seeing the brightest region it contains. Daniel Webster said, 'I shall enter on no encomium upon Massachusetts: she needs none. There she is; behold her, and judge for yourselves. There is her history. The world knows it by heart.'[120] I have a love for New England – a very strong affection – and shall be quite sorry to leave without seeing her and without making friends with some of the real noble Americans who live there. You see we have turned the corner of our journey and are on our road home again, coming up rivers instead of going down.

We have had a delightful two days on the Alabama River. Found some delightful friends on board and I became very friendly with the Captain who is also owner of that vessel and others. He is very anxious to find out that I am a relation of his wife's. Her name is Jane Smith, an Englishwoman. Twenty-five or thirty years ago she ran away to America, having married a Mr. Henderson without her parents' consent. She was a young girl and has never heard of them since. Her mother was a Monteith – she (the mother) was great friends with some Nightingales and knew Ld. Byron.

I told the Captain I would let him know if Aunt Patty could prove us any relation, as he was very anxious – neither he nor his wife having any relations in the world and only two children.

His name is Cloudis, a noble old fellow who began life at ten with a little brother of eight to keep and did keep him and himself, too, and now is in an influential position. The brother died, having made 100,000 dollars. This is not an unusual story here, but I have not seen any men in America I have liked better than this captain and the Mississippi captain.

They are both of the Mr. Gratton type: jolly, honest-looking but not to so high a degree as J.G.

The Alabama country we have seen from the river is very pleasant always, sometimes beautiful – sandy ridges of hill and rich plains between, where cotton is cultivated. Alabama is not rich enough for sugar. The sugar country is swamp. The cotton will grow well even on a poor sandy soil. We saw many pleasant little towns nestling in fir woods on the slopes of hills, and plantations with their rows of huts and the great house at some distance with trees and gardens and the picturesque cotton gins and little wharfs by the river.

One plantation we passed where all the negro huts had been burnt down a few nights before. Captain Cloudis told me that the big house was haunted. No one could live there since a wicked planter who was very cruel to his slaves had died in it.

Sunday, 28 February. At twelve o'clock went into the African Baptist Church close by. The preacher, a black man, was in the midst of the history of John. He related it in a very picturesque and vivid manner. He gave a very touching account of John as a very old man: 'Too old even to walk to his church to preach, being carried in and always preaching the same thing, "Little children, love one another," until the people were tired of the old man and his sermons and wanted something new as you often do, my brethren, and I tell you there is nothing new – it is an old story and you must take, etc. etc.'

I went again at seven in the evening and heard the same preacher and singing. Some voices were exquisite. I asked about the singers and find it is a free family who lead and have all fine voices. The minister thanked me for going. They always seem so thankful for a sympathizing face.

Afterwards they made a collection for building a new church and school room. I saw dollar notes and cent bits pouring in and could not help adding a bit. I always wish I had money when I visit these churches. They seem to me to give more comfort to negroes than anything else. In fact, it is their only mutual improvement association and I give my little mites with real pleasure.

The church is in mourning for an old black preacher lately dead. Black is hung over everything. The pulpits and curtains behind (all black) and the black preacher in black coat looked very diabolic. The evening sermon was not remarkable except for being very short: 'My brethren, I can only say a very few words to you because it is half past seven, and by the rules of the town we must stop at eight o'clock.'

The voices of the negroes are beautiful. Some day great singers will come out of that people. They sing all the negro melodies and hymns about the street, putting in musical sounds at the end of the verses which are peculiar – not yells or cries but allied and very effective. On board the steamboats they imitate musical instruments very well – so well that for the first time I thought it was an instrument, though I could not conceive what.

I often think of Longfellow's 'Negro singing at night.'[121] Sometimes when I hear them sing, the thought of slavery –

what it really is – makes me so utterly miserable. – One can do nothing – nothing – and I see little hope. It makes me wring my hands with anguish sometimes. So utterly helpless to help –

There are seven slaves in this house. Not one can read. They work all day and all Sundays, rarely go to church or out at all. The girl of thirteen who waits on us is a nice girl but dulled by overwork and oh, so tired every night.

The other day near where I was drawing in the forest, were two old women slowly picking out the moss for mattresses. We went up and talked to them. One could speak a little French. I said, 'How much do you get?' 'We get *nothing – we pay away our wages*, but we are old so they set us to this.' Near in a clearing we saw a black man ploughing up the light sandy soil very briskly. I asked him what crop, etc. He said for maize and melons between. I said, 'Who are you working for?' 'For myself. I hire this bit of land,' and I am sure by his clothes and well-to-do aspect he will get on.

Here there are very few free people of colour. The negroes tell me it is hardly worth while to be free – the laws are so hard on them now. If they stay in the state of Alabama (and I think here, too) they must have a nominal owner and go up to be registered at certain times and comply with all sorts of vexatious regulations, some of which are expensive.

I saw at Montgomery a bill saying *'free boy Will'* was to be hired out as a slave because he had not registered on the right day; was fined and unable (or unwilling) to pay the fine.

That reminds me of the next poster 'Great Grizzly bear of California,' etc. etc. etc., *'clergymen admitted gratis.'* The advertisements are very curious here: a great many about slaves and runaways, and as many about fortune tellers.

In the steamboat on the Alabama there was a cabin set apart for the coloured people and there I went for a little repose from the noise and bother of the ladies' cabin. One day watched a black girl dress a white baby. This was one of the drollest sights I ever saw and took three-quarters of an hour. The child was very pretty and very obstinate and would not put a leg or an arm into anything, so the black nurse had to take it by surprise. This she did in the most dramatic manner. She began by singing and so got one garment on and there stuck, then she begged me to show my little rabbit (Aunt Julia's wedding present), so I did and the trousers were tugged on while the child was enchanted with bunny. Then the nurse began to cry and to act out being hurt and while the child was consoling her, she whipt on the flannel petticoat. After that she began to play on a comb, then she sang and then she acted animals and cried and sang again. They are capital nurses and I believe the children often like them better than their mothers. This black girl was a jolly girl but so queer – Suddenly in the midst of her operations she stopped short and, whispering to me in the most confidential manner, said, 'Isn't the beefsteak awful?' I burst out laughing and said, 'What do you mean?' 'Why at dinner, and I can't eat it unless it is *well cooked and very tender*.' She was not starved – very few domestic slaves are. Sometimes on the plantations they suffer for want of food.

When we first came here eight days ago we went into the principal hotel and there (in consequence of bad weather) stayed two days and saw the society – which was much stupider than that you would find in a Hastings Hotel and about the same proportion of consumptive people. We then came to this boarding house where we see society a strata lower, but we have a good large airy room for writing and painting and so are well off, and at meals it is amusing to see the creatures. One evening the ladies sent for me to come into the drawing room and I went – and I don't think I shall go again.

This place (Savannah) is 6° of latitude south of Algiers and yet we have ice half an inch thick this morning the second of March. The changes are very great here. I pity the consumptive people. I fear I shall not get any painting out of doors now, but I have had three delicious days.

I am rather afraid of snakes in these woods but my doctor goes first and beats the woods with his stick, and I am very careful where I sit. But there are great difficulties in getting sketches in America – more than in any country I ever was in – so mine will be very valuable.

2 March.
My dear Aunty and Mr. Gratton,

I wish you would write to me. *Not one line have I had from either of you since I came away six months ago,* and every day I have written something for you all at home. It is more than a month since I have had a line from Blandford Square and more than two since I had a scrap from Bell.[122] I hope the letters have been lost. If I did not think so I should not continue to write, of course.

I send you my journal enclosed. Please send it to 5B. Squre. to Pater. I write as much as I can without blinding myself. My doctor is very well and sends his particular kind souvenirs to you both.

Now the winter has gone. Spring has come. I am very sorry – I don't like the time to go so quickly. The flowers in the woods are very beautiful here: three sorts of violets – one very big with a leaf [illustration] like this, another milk-white (which grows in water), ferns are coming up gloriously. I never see them in great beauty without saying to my Doctor I wish we could grab them all for your new house. Are you really going to move? If so, joy to the new house and long and happy life in it is the prayer of your affect. Bar.

3 March. Yesterday afternoon we walked out four miles and a half along the plank road into the forest. It was wonderfully beautiful – the trees immense and such a jungle of creepers of all sorts and moss matted and heaped together in the wildest manner.

Sometimes the trees met over the road and the moss hung down like gothic ornaments and above, a roof of greenery. It was very picturesque to see the horsemen (black and white) with guns and pistols and coloured harness and ribbons riding through the chequered light. Sometimes we met two or three carts with emigrants – and then a party of Germans singing as they drove, carrying with them their paint pots to paint signs for all the towns they drove through. Then we came upon a young German reading in the forest out of a little leather book (either the Bible or a classic). He had a good face and we saluted him as we passed.

I thoroughly enjoy these fir forests. They are not dreadful

to stay in like the cypress forests and here there are other trees – fine magnolias and bay trees whose leaves are lined with silver, and in the wind and sun looked wonderfully lovely.

It is very cold. I am glad we are going to stay here a month before going to Washington because cold prevents me from working very much.

Wednesday–Thursday, 3–4 March.
My dear Pater,
I wish you would write to me. I write to you almost every day a bit and send the letters one a week, but it is like talking in the dark and getting no answer. So this week I send you Ben and bears,[123] hoping you will acknowledge it with thanks. It is certainly the best specimen of American art I have yet seen.

I sent you some stupid papers to show you what Southern papers are. I was so hard up for English news that I gave a shilling for the *London Illus:* to read about our Princess. I am sure the man who said to the young Prince who was crying, 'God bless you, my dear boy' was Mr. Gratton.[124]

If you write to the Doctor a scrap he will always answer and tell you how I am, but perhaps you have answered his letter and it has been lost. This damned post is reason enough for not visiting America.

I have nothing to say but it is very cold, ice every day. It was a good thing we did not come north (even so far north as this) before.

I must wait two months before I can see Boston and Niagara. I will write you very particular accounts of all those places you have seen so that you may see them again.

4 March. I sent off a letter to Mr. Gratton yesterday which you will get in time.

Here in this house the cowhide is used to the black back of my nice Clara who works so hard – isn't it devilish? I was near going down and making a row, as Aunt Julia and Don Quixote would have done – but on second thought feel certain I should make things worse, so I consoled Clara with bull eyes and wait my time to put in a word if I can to the Mistress of this boarding house (who by the bye is a Northern woman and the

Southerners all say they make the worst masters and mistresses, and next in honour come the French. The worst cases of cruelty are French because when bad the French have a prodigious capacity of devilry. But generally the slaves are treated in French families more as the family than in American and are taught more).

I find we have ten negroes in this house. They are 'hired out' to the Mistress – a bad look-out for slaves to be hired out to a boarding house.

By the time you get this I shall be close at home – that is within twelve or thirteen days of Blandford Square. (Write *P.O. Washington*), but I hope you will not expect me at home until I have seen Niagara, for I shall never come to America again, never as long as I live, I hope. I do not like it well enough. 'Though it is more worth seeing than all other countries.

We have had here delightful walks (the Doctor and I) and have seen such beautiful creatures – birds of all sorts: creepers, perchers, waders, divers. Nothing so lovely as the bluebird. One day we saw fifty of them with their azure backs and wings flying, glancing in the sunlight or picking up seeds. The Doctor is perfectly happy watching birds. I never saw any one with such a love of animals. He is just the creature to ramble with and never minds any trials of temper the incidents of travel or BLS expose him to. Audubon[125] must have been a happy man. This is the country for a naturalist. The woods swarm with live things. It is too cold to paint, so I ramble in the woods. Though it freezes, it is warm in the fir forests and delicious to ramble about.

Friday, 5 March. I have just heard the first news of Bell's illness.[126] We shall go northward and I shall be ready to go home when sent for. Write to E. Blackwell to telegraph for me.[127] She will know where I am always.

We wait for the second letter as the first was lying a week at the hotel before they gave it me. The postmaster against my express orders sent it.

I am *very well* – never better in my life – but very anxious to hear of you all.

Your affectionate Bar.

Dr. Bodichon sends all sorts of kind messages and wishes he could be of use. Let him know if he can, but he will write to you about it.

Sunday, 7 March. I went to the Methodist Church. It is a pleasant-looking white Noah's-Ark-looking building – very large, very white, very cheerful, with windows all round. I heard singing as I approached. I went in and stayed an hour. The minister, a slave and very black negro, gave a good sermon on the Communion. It was not remarkable. In the evening I went to my Baptist Church close by and heard another slave preach. The regular minister (also a slave) whom I heard last Sunday was not there. I asked a few questions about him of a very old man who seemed to be an authority. He said the minister could read and write and had studied. I asked how he could study if he worked all day. He said he studied at night and of course he can't do as well as white men who have all their time, but 'he *worries and scuffles* and so gets a little learning, I think. The Lord [watches over] them, for the black preachers are nearly all slaves,' etc.

I found the congregation as polite as usual but the negroes are more reserved in their manners here than at New Orleans. They look well and happy. I have talked to many and cannot say they are unhappy even when their circumstances are unhappy. For instance, a woman today told me she was the property of a gentleman in the country who hires her out to a white washerwoman here in Savannah. Here she always stays unless she is going to have a child then she goes to the plantation and stays until the child can toddle, then out to work again. She has had five children but never sees them except under these circumstances. 'Well,' I said, 'how do you get along?' 'Oh, splendidly – of course must get along, you see, there ain't no other way – splendidly!' Sometimes I meet faces which are tragedies to look on, but generally these are mulattoes.

This is a very flourishing pleasant city. I like it very much. John Oglethorpe, the noble Englishman who founded it, had good taste. The history of the founding of Savannah is very interesting.

Friday, 12 March.
Savannah.

In the beautiful fir wood where I have been four or five times to paint I have heard a pleasant voice singing hymns. Yesterday the singer appeared, a young negro girl, very slight and small, but she says eighteen years old.

She and her little sister of four or five sang to me Negro songs and hymns. It seems more natural to negroes to sing than to talk. A boy came up and sang too. After some conversation I found out this boy was much given to running away and was often whipped for it. The girl said she would never do anything so wicked. I was very much amused with these children and they were amused at me. 'Never saw anybody like you.' They were not sure whether I was Indian or not.

They peeled off the inner bark on the fir and chewed it like tobacco, but the girl said, 'If Master seed us do that he'd whipt us because it spoils the teeth.'

The boy was sent for to bring a cart and horse to his master directly, but he very coolly put it off in a way which would have lost a boy his place in England.

This fir wood is a lovely place to settle in, healthy and beautiful. I can hardly imagine any pleasanter country for emigrants to come to than the neighbourhood of Savannah.

I heard the strokes of the axe, and the trees falling at intervals as I drew, all day, and I understood the pleasure of cutting a square hole in the dense wood, building a house and making a market-garden, as the young man was doing with the certainty of gaining a good living.

March 12.
Savannah.

My dear Pater and Nanny,

We leave Savannah today, and I suppose this day week we shall be in Washington certainly, perhaps before. I have waited for letters but received *none*. The last three days no post has been in, in consequence of the stoppage of the trains by a snow tempest. I am thankful we did not start as I wished last Friday (5th). We should have been snowed up. Doctor said with that icy wind from the North he was sure it was not safe to travel, and I hoped for a letter every day. The last two days it has been quite hot, so we hope to be able to get north without any trouble.

We go by the Savannah River to Augusta and then take rail to Wilmington and Washington.[128]

I wrote last Friday (5th) and to Aunt Julia two days ago. Perhaps in this snow the letters are lost. I hope to heaven your letters to me are not lost but most likely some are, for in accidents on the rail the mail bags are often stolen or lost. It makes me *very anxious* to be within a shorter distance (even if, as I am hoping, Bell is better and there is no immediate necessity to go home).

I do not feel sure we shall get to Washington in a week. There has been no winter and these sudden storms in March are, they say, the worst storms and the bitterest cold of the year. It is so hot today that I hope the spring has come.

We go by boat because it saves a long railway journey on the same line we came, and because after these riverboats we can get into the rail quite fresh and go on without fatigue for a long shake on the trains.

Love to all. Yr. affect. Bar.

My doctor sends his kindest regards to every one of you.

> *Saturday, 13 March.*
> *On board the Swan.*

Savannah River. Lovely summer day, glorious woods each side of us of oaks, maples, magnolias, firs and other trees. Last night we ran into some half dozen sand banks and five or six trees, and I rushed out to see what was to be seen and saw nothing but stars in the sky and sparks from our engine against the woods, black on each side, and a great grey tree or two leaning over us with the mournful moss looking very dreary and ghostly in the dim light. Where we wooded in the night it was a beautiful picture – flaring flambeaus of fir tied on the rafts, dropping fire into the black water.

14 March.   The river is very monotonous as everything is in America. The trees are like a wall, so thick that it is difficult to see more than the first row. We went into one of the woods this morning at seven o'clock when the vessel stopped to wood.

There we found six or eight negroes and three or four white men congregated round the fire where they had slept all night to guard the cotton, which was lying by the river to be exported by our boat. The trees were very high and the river here wide with a wooded island in it – very picturesque indeed. The red-headed woodpecker was quite close to us in the trees and the big black crows sailing overhead with their loud caw caw. These crows are magnificent birds and very intelligent when tamed (if half the stories they tell me here are true). We must bring one home. My Doctor believes all they say because he tamed one, which was of a sagacity marvellous. We talked to a young man who had come from Canada and whose father was French. He was quite a refined polite gentleman though rough in dress.

We land very often though there is not a house to be seen – nothing but forest primeval, forest everlasting. The fact is that behind the forest lowland in which the river runs there is high land on either side – with cotton plantations and gentlemen's houses. Many planters and their families come on board this boat, it being their property supported for their convenience; to us it is something like being their guest. I have talked a good deal with them but found nothing remarkable, except the dress and manner of one young lady who was the most perfectly *bien mise* of any American I have seen, but when she spoke the charm vanished. They all thought it a great hardship to live on the fare of the boat, which I thought excellent. I think the ladies are greedy.

I found some negro women who talked very pleasantly and were very anxious to hear about our Princess and her marriage. They said, *'we love the Queen of England so much that if she were to come and see us we should go mad with joy.'* I say it is a glorious thing for our Queen to be loved so and I wish she knew it. The negroes here believe the Queen is their friend and would free them if she could. I hope this is true. I was very glad I had too a hearty affection for 'our Royal Family,' and could describe the whole group as I saw them last at the Oratorio at the Crystal Palace.[129] One young mulatress said 'I hear the Princess wore no hoops at her marriage. Is it so?' I said most likely it was so.

All these women had the wish to be free. One of our party

was free and said, 'I'd rather live all my days on a crust of bread as I am than be a slave. I was born free.' She got ten dollars a month on the boat and presents besides.

Sunday, 14 March. At 4 p.m., arrived at Augusta. As the train did not start until eight p.m. we walked about town – a struggling town of immensely wide streets, as usual, of villas with gardens. The river is beautiful but the country not interesting at all. We went on board to have tea with the Captain and then the black sailors carried our boxes to the station close by the river and we went off. All night long 'rattle his bones, over the stones' rang in my ears. The train made a horrid noise. Sun came up and still rattle her bones and smoke and stifle and on and on through the sand and the firs, until three o'clock p.m. Monday we got to Wilmington and crossed the river and settled down to wash off the dust and grime of the dirtiest journey I ever made. We saw nothing but the same forests and sand, and now and then a clearing with a circular saw sawing up firs and a few men at work raising huts. The fir trees for miles were skinned of their bark to let the resin run out. This is one of the great articles of commerce about here.[130]

The people in the train were a queer mixture – rough men and ladies in expensive skirts and bright silks came in and got out at little log hut stations and went off in 'buggies' through the woods to farms and plantations; young ladies coming, or coming from the towns on visits; bearded young men who looked like pickpockets and were very likely, as on every hand you are warned by placarders (or more pathetically, by sufferers) to take care of purses and chains, as the thieves are the cleverest in the world and when once a thing is lost there is no hope of any police help here.

Everywhere the same liberty and audacity – fine plan of constitution and government, finely planned railway and hotel – but not well carried out by the people. The ideas are fine, the execution almost always defective.

I read on board the *Swan* a great part of the history of 1775 and 6[131]—what a noble history it is; what fine men they were. I do not see such men in America now and I doubt if the women of this time would have helped them now as those women did, in war and privations of all sorts. 'I think the women have degenerated,' three of four Americans have said, and I fear it is true. With the exception of six or eight eccentric women I have met, the mass are very far below the mass of women in England in health of soul and body.

Negro women are much more agreeable to me. I left our little Clara at Savannah with real sorrow. In two weeks I had seen a great deal of her and found her very intelligent and affectionate. She was so sorrowful to part from me that she could not say one word and put herself behind the door perfectly quiet. She told me she had no one in the world who cared for her. Her father was alive but she never saw him. Slave owners may say what they like but families *are* separated – when not is the exception. The lies I have read! here in newspapers and *Cabins* (answers to *Uncle Tom* which deluge the South, where the original is not to be found on any table). It is always asserted that the families are kept together and the reverse is a rare and sad occurrence. Why, every week in New Orleans hundreds are sold from Virginia and Maryland and it is rarely that a family is sold altogether – father, mother and children (*never* I was going to say, but it is sometimes the case). There is one slave-dealer in New Orleans who does not sell slaves without consulting them as to their likes and dislikes. He asks them whether they will like such and such a master. This I heard on very good authority, but mentioned as a very curious and solitary instance. When I was talking to these negro women on board the *Swan*, as usual they said, 'You must not speak loud, you must speak low or you will get into trouble.' An English lady and gentleman had to leave New Orleans merely for talking abolition, and at Mobile a Unitarian minister only escaped tar and feathers by flight, because in the pulpit he made some allusions to abolition doctrines.

I say I am not an Abolitionist. I am not. What I wish is for gradual freedom: *freedom for the free blacks first in all the states, freedom to buy themselves, freedom to educate themselves.*

Instead of any tendency to ameliorate the condition of the slave I see nothing but increasing barbarity in the laws and firmer barriers raised against the certain encroachment of the universal spirit of freedom. Here, as in Europe, laws to stifle this spirit increase in severity. Despotism seems dominant, but in spite of appearances there are more souls alive to the idea of self-government than ever before.

My feeling against the whites of the South is for their wickedness in trying to brutify instead of elevate the African race. My hate for it is hate not against slave owners but against all in America who would exclude the dusky skinned from the light of knowledge and the blessings of freedom which here all the white race so abundantly enjoys.

We are both struck by the intelligence and general agreeableness of the negroes and mulattoes. The race is not so low in the human scale as I supposed before I came here. Probably the field hands are inferior. I take Olmsted's account as true, for I have not seen much of plantation life.[132] When I am in the country I paint, and it is only in the towns I see the negroes.

Tuesday, 16 March.
Wilmington.

My dear Pater,

We shall be in Washington in twenty hours now unless I am very tired and we stop at Weldon,[133] which we can do if we like. The railways are very good for that. You can stop where you like and go on next day or any day for six days after you have taken your ticket.

I wrote three letters from Savannah. I am very anxious to get to my letters at Washington. I shall write from thence to you.

Best love to Bell and Nanny and all. Doctor sends always his very kindest regards to you and he says I am to say I look *very well* in spite of our journey. I am quite well. Yr. Bar.

March 16. We have walked round the town and seen all there is to see which is nothing. The town is on a slight elevation in the marshy country which extends to the sea. The streets are all sandy and today, as it is like a bright hot June day in England, it is unpleasant to walk in the hot white sand so we are glad to wait here in this cool room up on the veranda (where there are ten or twelve negroes of all ages singing and chattering) until we go off to the railway for Washington.

It is very hot today, blazing sun. I hope as we go North it will continue.

On the 16th we left Wilmington and rattled on in the heat and sun through the everlasting fir forest, until the sun went down yellow and hot behind the sandy hills and dried-up trees. On we went smothered in the bituminous smoke of the fir wood burnt in feeding the engine, until suddenly out of the darkness we went dashing through a region of fire: the resinous fir trees stood columns of flames, the fire ran along on the ground, fire dropped down from the branches, trees stood alive with red sparks, trees toppled down, blackened and smoking. A wilderness hissing and crackling. Poor birds! dearest grey squirrels! Where are you? We are gone! Our giant has dragged us into the haunts of the human and no time is left me to wait for the birds and beasties ejected.

At twelve that night we stopped at Weldon, I being dead tired.

Wednesday, 17 March. Left Weldon which is rather a pretty place, hilly ground and a river running madly and muddily through sand and firs. Richmond[134] too seems pretty, but it was nearly dark and I only saw from the awful viaduct the foam of the rapids dimly, down far below us.

At Aquia Creek[135] we took boat and arrived at Washington five a.m. *18th* of *March*, after a hot journey made fifty times more fatiguing by the obstinate love of being stifled which possesses these American ladies. In the hotels I met some of the most disagreeable young ladies I ever saw in my life – ignorant and audacious beyond any Englishwoman's ideas of audacity. Good Lord defend us, how they all play on pianos! Instant the train stops they dart to ladies' rooms and play like mad. Sometimes (well, generally) too much like the railway rattle and smash. They are fatiguing women, *wery*.

Thursday, 18 March.
Washington.

My dearest Pater and Georgie,

Many thanks for your messages and letters most thankfully received this hot dusty day. No fear of cold – it is hot, rather too hot – so hot I felt ready to drop when I got the letters. Thankful to hear Bell is better. I hope she will soon write to me. We are here with friends, not slave-owning friends, my dear Julia, but friends of the Spring sort. We have two rooms in a magnificent phalanstery,[136] as my Doctor says. We have a good many good things. Fine view, good food, good beds and good people which we enjoy all the more for having lived without in the South.

18 March.
Washington.

My dearest Aunty and Mr. Gratton,

Got your letter today – uncommon glad. I thought you both had behaved brutally to me. My Doctor thanks you for all your kind wishes and returns them to you with interest. This is a jolly place! Beautiful city! I think of myself and my father and mother here two years – it is a curious life.

We shall come home after seeing something of Canada and Niagara and Boston. Ours has been a very successful tour. No accident as yet and no loss.

I wish you would take a house in a place where you had a bit of garden. *It is such a pleasure,* even if smoky.

I am very glad of the fern and moss resurrection. I have collected seeds for Mr. Gratton hoping he would have a garden. Dr. and I have been always on the lookout for *queerosities.*

You must be satisfied with scraps of letters because *I write all I can.* I am so sorry the Duke of Devonshire is dead![137] I know you both were.

The Americans are the most curious mixture! They do things on the most magnificent scale. Their hotels are like towns, or rather, palaces. For 10 shillings a day you have splendid drawing rooms (public), every delicacy in the way of eating, including ices after every dinner! But one day is enough for me, for unless I get a good working room I don't care for life. At Savannah we got what we wanted for 28 shillings a week each. Here we must give twice as much.

I think we shall enjoy Washington very much indeed.

My Southern sketches are going to be exhibited here at an art gallery. Fourteen of mine are exhibiting at Philadelphia, Boston, etc. in the English Ex.[138]

Best love, your loving Bar.

Monday, 22 March. On Saturday we had the very pleasantest day (as far as seeing clever and agreeable people goes) which we have enjoyed in America.

First let me say a word about Barbara Smith, particularly for John Thomas who has said three or four times in his letters that it is not correct to call myself Barbara Smith Bodichon. I believe he is wrong as a matter of law. I do not think there is any law to oblige a woman to bear the name of her husband at all, and probably none to prevent keeping the old name. To use it is very useful, for I have earned a right to Barbara Smith and am more widely known than I had any idea of, and constantly my card with my name on it is useful in getting me friends. Dr. says he should think it folly for me to use his name except as a convenience in society, and if we have a line of English descendants they will be Bodichon-Smiths. He would be sorry to add to French population.

There is here a sister of Ellen Bracher (an old schoolfellow of ours at Miss Woods') married to the gentleman of the art gallery where my Southern sketches are. When she saw my card she remembered me quite well and is a pleasant acquaintance for us.

Thank Mr. Sylvester[139] for his letter to Professor Henry. We were there on Saturday. I like Prof. H. exceedingly and the Smithsonian Institute is an enchanting place over which the amiable Professor reigns like a king. There were some – people there at dinner and two quite –.[140] One of them was old Peale the artist who painted Washington from life.[141] I talked to him. Dr. talked to the Professor about races. At 8 we went to Dr. Bayley's.[142] He is the editor of the *National Era* (I send you some numbers) and his house the headquarters of the liberal party here. I never met so many agreeable men in one evening in my life. There were Senators and Members and writers and travellers and all as pleasant as if in their own homes. I had a long conversation with Parker[143] who has been twenty-four years in China and told me more about Chinese moeurs than I should have read in twelve volumes. Mr. Chase, friend of M. Fullar and Mary Ware interested me much.

Of course there was intense excitement about Kansas and Douglas's speech. The political men had fine –[144] looked honest and good. In fact all the people there assembled were a noble specimen of America. Dr. B. had a long talk with Mr. Alexander who is really Lord Stirling you know.[145] He is a pleasant and clever man and has an office in the Patent Office and so gets his living. What a fine place the Patent Office is![146] In fact I am enchanted with Washington and so tired that I can't write any more.

Wednesday, 7 April.
Avenue House, Washington.

My dearest Pater,

I have received your letter saying we must go to Quebec and that I may draw on you. *Thanks!* But I shall have enough of my own I hope, without drawing on you, and I am sure you have enough to pay for Algerian expenses![147] I am very much relieved to hear that Bell is better. My doctor knows the people of the place they have gone to, and says they are honest good people. He is very glad all the French have been so good, especially glad his countryman and woman M. & Me. Tousilainte are such good friends to Nanny. We are going to write to them and to dear old Mouton and to good, clever Me. Girault.

Our friends the Bayleys have left Washington and we should leave on the 9th, but it is again so cold that we decided to stay until the 16th; then to Baltimore (one hour by rail) and then on the 17th to Philadelphia, where we shall be when you get this letter. On the 1st May we shall be in New York where we shall stay as short a time as possible just to greet our many friends and spend a day or two with the Springs at the Union.[148] Probably on the 8th of May we shall be at Boston, but if the weather is very cold we shall delay for I do believe the cold wind and hot sun are the enemies to be avoided. I always walk with an umbrella even on icy days for the sun's rays are pricking like hot fir's needles.

Yesterday we started at half past seven, walked to the Potomac, took a steamer and went to Mt. Vernon. We were very much interested to see the walks, the daily haunts and last resting place of George Washington. I am very glad he had such a pleasant retreat. It is a comfortable place, very like an old English house, and as it was built two hundred years ago was probably built, every stone of it, by Englishmen. Please ask Willy to plant carefully the enclosed seeds, or if Georg is with you let her plant them in a pot. They are from the garden. The little fern must go to Mr. Gratton immediately or if he has no house you must put it under a glass.

Mount Vernon is going to ruin very fast; the owners are poor and going to ruin too I suppose. The ladies of America are getting up a subscription to buy it. It is worth (they say) 20,000 dollars and the proprietors ask 200,000! cool.[149]

Last night I went to the Levee at the White House with some ladies in this house and Mr. Philp. My Doctor would not go. I found it intensely amusing. The people were nearly all in evening costume, some well dressed but most gaudy and shabby, a few were in working clothes and a few ladies in bonnets. I saw the Turkish Admiral and suite, generals and diplomats, etc. Of course I shook hands with Mr. Buchanan and Miss Lane his niece, who does the honours of his house very well.[150] She is very pretty, fresh as an English woman and dresses in good taste. In fact the whole arrangements were good, simple and elegant. I think there were eight or nine hundred people. We went in an omnibus and walked back, so that it was a very easy matter. You might have accomplished it without difficulty.

Tonight we go to Mrs. Johnson's and meet some abolitionists (M.P.'s) and tomorrow to Professor Henry's. The Doctor sends his best regards to you.

Love to Georgie, yr. affect. Bar.

Sunday, 18 April.
Philadelphia.

My dearest Pater,

In case you should not receive my letter from Baltimore, please tell John Thornely I draw today £150. Mr. Wm. Mill of New York will give me the money as I want it. I wrote to John Thornely yesterday. I sent a long journal for you to Bessie from Washington on 16th.

Yesterday as we rattled along in the rail, about two o'clock we came to a ploughed field, nothing particular to look at, and in it was standing a stick and (nothing particular to look at) on this stick was a white flag. That was Mason and Dixon's line[151] that was the boundary between the Slave States and the Free, between Delaware and Pennsylvania – and though the air did not change or the land look happier as we passed and came on this side, I can tell you my feelings changed so much that it seemed to me as if everything was better, brighter, truer, at once. I like Philadelphia at once but I do not think we shall be so comfortable here as in our delightful rooms at Washington and among those pleasant people. I had a charming window there to paint at. Here we are in a dark street and probably shall go in a week to Raritan Bay Union where we shall be at home with the good Springs, Welds and the rest.

We were sorry to leave the Washingtonians who were so very hospitable and cordial to us. I do not think I mentioned Mrs. Heiss who was in the same house with us. She and I had a great deal of talk together. Her husband was editor of a paper and as all Americans seemed to be a major in the Army. Mr. and Mrs. Heiss have lived in Central America and California and are going to live at –.[152] She is a weak little body but a plucky little soul and I like her very much. She has a liking for eccentric women, and told me of three women who edit newspapers with extraordinary ability (of one – Mrs. Swishelm – more anon).[153] She admired much a young woman who left home to travel and learn all about Central America, and who wrote and studied and wandered. On one occasion when there was war in Nicaragua (I think) she came to Mrs. Heiss and for the sake of being under a safe roof lived herself as Mrs. H.'s cook. She had plenty of pluck and power of adapting herself to circumstances. Seeing the want of women, she proposed to several hundred of the 'Sons of Temperance' in California to go back to New England and bring them out an equanent number of 'Daughters of Temperance.' She is now engaged in this work, more of her also when I get particulars. There is a stir among the women over here, and you may imagine all these indications interest me very much indeed.

I went to the Unitarian Chapel this morning and heard Mr. Furness[154] preach an excellent sermon on contentment from Paul's Epistle to the Philippians. He says (I forget the text) that in whatever place God may place him, he is there with content. He was in prison when he said this and on this Mr. Furness preached for an hour admirably. The sum was this:

that to be always contented with all external circumstances of life, a profound internal *discontent* with evil is necessary and a fixed determination to fight against the evil and make the good triumph.

The singing was very beautiful. It is a real pleasure to go to church in America.

? April. Philadelphia. After dinner Dr. and I took a long walk in search of a better abode but found nothing. Mr. Furness and Mr. Mott (Lucretia Mott's son)[155] say it is impossible to get into a quiet house – all are of the same pattern. As we neared our hotel I stopped at a church and went in just to take what might come by hazard. I found it was Presbyterian. Very full of well dressed people (not the tip-top fashionable). *All* the congregation were singing just as they do at Henry Beecher's, which after all is better than the Unitarian fashion of having the music done for them. The minister was an old man and he preached a very interesting sermon on the different characters of the twelve Apostles dwelling on their faults and making them individual men. I hardly ever heard a sermon in which there was so much thought and study. He gave three or four different readings to some passages and seemed confidently to count on his congregation's interest in the different Greek words used for *hell*. This sermon was one of a series of afternoon discourses on Luke, I believe.

After the sermon the minister gave out that three services would be held in the week and mentioned his joy to see different sects joining in these prayer meetings. This is the almost universal attribute of the revivals – all are invited to meet together and pray.

Sometimes they pray, I grant, for the conversion of Theodore Parker,[156] but after all it is a good thing, this proselyting spirit. I like it. In England people are very different about spreading what they hold to be true, or perhaps they don't feel sure that anything they hold is true.

I was glad I went in, for it confirmed me in my opinion that the churches of America are far superior to the churches of England or any other country. Certainly the free system is a wonderful success and surprises me more than I can express.

I did not expect to see the ministers of religion so respected and so highly respectable a body. They hold a higher place in the respect and affection of the people than the ministers of religion in England.

Saturday, 17 April.   Received your letter of April 1st offering £250 to finish our journey. Very much obliged, dear Pater, but hope I shall not want it. You see, Mr. Neill (who is Unitarian and known to the Thornelys and Martineaus) will let us have money in bits and do anything for us in the world. I chose to make Mr. Neill our friend and banker because he is English and we can return his kindness by inviting him to see us on some of his journeys to London.

We have left the hotel and come into a boarding house where are medical students, and we pay £1 each a week – two rooms, excellent food and a fine drawing-room to receive visitors in, which I have almost to myself. Five dollars each is rather different from the Southern prices!

Tuesday, 20 April.
Dear Pater,

It is very cold here and there is no sign of spring yet: we seem to have gone back in the seasons. But we are with warm-hearted 'friends' and so can bear the cold wind. We are both well and send our best love to all.

Your Bar.

Dear Georgie, *I hope my letters are kept or copied.* Many thanks for your weekly letters.

Your affect. B.

20th.   A cold, pelting rain and as dreary a day as ever I saw. At half past eight we set out to walk to the N. Pennsylvania Rail Station to go to City Lane to see Lucretia Mott.[157] At the Station we saw a 'Rockaway'[158] standing in the pelting rain, a fat little horse and well-to-do-looking old 'friend.' We had no doubt been expected in spite of the detestable weather and this was Friend Mott, no doubt come for us. Yes. So in we got and drove through what must be a very pretty park which encloses the villas of Friend Thomas Mott and some of his relations.

Arrived at a pleasant-looking country house, we are received at the door by one of the four daughters of the house and led into a pretty, bright-looking room, and Lucretia Mott greets us as cordially as if we were really 'Friend Barbara' and 'Friend Bodichon.' She looks just like a picture. I never saw such a beautiful old lady, really beautiful and so exquisite in her dress, like a pearl. I fell in love with her immediately. She looks 'full of grace' in every sense of the word. I do not wonder her preaching has stirred so many souls, her aspect is eloquent, her smile full of good things. She seems to be full of vigour and looks in perfect health, though I believe she is seventy years old. She asked me about Lady Byron,[159] Friend Elizabeth Reid and Julia Smith and spoke of them, all three with great regard, especially Friend Elizabeth Reid. She put her hands on my shoulders and said how happy it made her to see that the young women of England were thinking about their rights and trying to do something for justice and freedom. She asked me about Eliza Ton and Bessie Parkes[160] and Mrs. J. Shill especially and I told her as well as I could the number of women and the principal powers on the side of *Women's Rights* in England. When she was in England (1840?), she says, the idea was scouted and no women she met in England dared to advocate the rights of women. She seemed absolutely to chuckle with glee to hear that we hold all that she and 'the Friends' advocate and only wait to claim the suffrage because it would be useless to try for it now. Massachusetts must make that move – and will, I believe – before many years are passed. So at least the women think.

It is a pleasure to see thoroughgoing reformers who are not poor – it is so rare to see rich people really given to reform ideas. When I see a rich woman like Lucretia Mott advocating a cause which is yet in the rotten-egg stage (I mean its advocates are apt to have rotten eggs and dirtier words thrown at them), I think there is some hope of the rich getting through the eye of the needle into heaven.

Lucretia Mott asked me many questions about the South and slavery, and I told her what I have told you of the wonderful eloquence of the black preachers, of the sales at N. Orleans, the general well-being of the coloured population (compared to white) in Louisiana, of the secret schools, and of the widespread knowledge among the slaves of the efforts made to emancipate.

Lucretia Mott showed me a mass of Woman's Right literature and I made my pick for the benefit of B.R.P. and M.H.,[161] and she showed me her books of notes for lectures with extracts and little quotations so nicely put together, and as we looked them over she gave me little accounts of the occasions on which they were used. She says all the Women's Rights conventions have been quiet, orderly and dignified and that the rumours of their vulgarity are absolutely unfounded. This Mr. Mott confirmed and said they were more orderly than conventions held by men.

Of course we had a nice dinner and no wine but delicious tea.

Bessie remembers Miss Pugh. She was there and her sister, and I was charmed with them. Fanny Priestly is coming to stay with them.

I was very happy that they had remarked one of my drawings – the 'sunset over corn and willow land' which was exhibited here in the English Ex: and now gone to Boston.

Please let Mrs. Reid know that I have seen her friends and how pleasant it was to me to feel a link between such good people.

My Doctor was delighted with the whole family as much as I was, and we drove away with good Friend Mott in the rockaway to the station in a most satisfied state of mind and soaking rain. Mrs. Howitt's niece Miss Harrison is going to marry into this society and I think she could not do better; Lucretia Mott is a heart. I wish we had in England ten thousand good as she.

Tomorrow we go to an anti-slavery meeting with Mrs. Mott and you shall hear what else we do. But I shall post this when we are in the town.

Sunday, 11 May.
Eaglewood School, Perth Amboy, N. Jersey.[162]
My dear Pater and all,

Thanks for letters of the 23d of April. I hope Georgie will be married by the time you get this. I send a letter to her by this mail, direct to 5 B. Sqre.

We have had a delightful week here. The children are gone home for a week so that we see more of the Welds[163] than we did and more of the few children left behind, and I can study the school better than when it is in full swing. We are both quite convinced that the system is answering perfectly well both for boys and girls, little and grown (for some of them are eighteen and nineteen years old).

I never saw such a satisfactory group of young people in my life. Mr. Weld is working out every day his principles of equal advantages for black or white or male or female.

It is one of the most beautiful sights in the world to see the affection the pupils have for him and he for them. He does everything with them – joined heart and soul in a *molasses candy-pull* which we all had in the kitchen the other night. By the bye, that is an institution of the country and very *peculiar*, too.

I had a very lovely walk with Mr. Weld one day this week in the cypress wood. Over the mossy ground encircled with the bluest violets and the whitest anemones I ever saw he discoursed on the excellent results of having boys and girls brought up together, and told me of the many testimonies given by the boys after they had left school to the admirable influence it had exerted. The school is only one part of the education influence of the place. The Springs[164] and the Kirklands live in the park and make a society which is quite an influence. Then the families in the Union House, Mrs. Birney and others (who are drawn together by affinity to the idea which governs the whole), made a group which I believe to be unique. Visitors from all parts of the world come down here and give lectures, readings, or whatever they can contribute to the Commonwealth of enjoyment or instruction.

The children are quite different from all other American children I have seen. They are full of fun and spirits, strong and healthy. I wish you could see Annie Tallman, a beautiful girl of eighteen. She has short curls, rosy cheeks, bright hazel eyes, and the expression of a young Hebe.[165] She is tall and slight and a real young athlete. She jumps three feet four inches like a deer and walks along a ladder hung only by her hands like an acrobat! All the girls practice gymnastics but she happens to be here for this week, so I go into the gymnasium with her and am never tired of seeing her exquisite grace and activity. In the pretty short dress she is a lovely picture. She learns Latin, Greek, mathematics and book-keeping etc., but she is only fond of music and she wishes to be a musician and go to Germany and study the violin so as to gain her own living. A granddaughter of Lucretia Mott is also a fine production of the school. She is a student and one of the most sensible girls I ever met in my life. Some of these girls will be heard of in the world, I am convinced.

But to go back to the walk with Mr. Weld. He took me through the woods, down the little ravine, up the hills by a path (no road) through evergreen cypress and other trees, to one point higher and more retired and more deeply wooded with evergreen shrubs and trees, and told me this part of the wood was their place to bury the dead and there already are six who have died here: four very old and two or three children.[166] There is no enclosure and only one grave has a fence round it. Most of them are only marked by a mound or trees or flowers. Of course this place has not been blessed by any other blessing than God's and all may lie there, however different in faith and life. We stood by Mr. Birney's grave and Mr. Weld told me how nobly he had lived, how hard his life had been at the time he gave freedom to his slaves, the constant risk of death, the daily struggle, the disappointments he had suffered, and how perfectly he had overridden all and had lived as he thought right and acquired so perfect peace and faith that dying was absolutely nothing to him.[167] He had some years back a paralytic stroke and for years was in a state which made death probable any day. Mrs. Birney was a wife worthy of him and now she seems to live with the perfect consciousness of his spirit being alive and near him. She is here and many of her grandchildren at school here.

We have had Gerrit Smith here (anti-slavery man etc.) and he is a magnificent man to look at, eloquent and kind, but does not impress me as one of the strong intellects of America.[168] Mrs. Farnham from California has been here.[169] She is a very remarkable woman. She was matron of Sing Sing Prison, New York, and has seen the worst women of all countries. She has also been active in the Society for sending girls from New York *west*. She is settled now in California and loves that country

intensely as all do who go there. It must be like Italy, rather
Algiers, in climate and beauty. She is the leader of the Woman's
Rights party in San Francisco and will certainly do work for I
never saw a more vigorous woman in my life. More of her
anon.

On Sunday our morning meeting was more than usually
interesting. Father Buffum read the chapter, Annie Tallman
played and we sang as usual.[170] Then Father Buffum gave
a regular old-style Quaker address. Then a brother of Mr.
Weld's (who does, I think the rough work of the Union) got
up and made a spirit speech, saying the spirits had come as
prophesied and warning us against the demons, etc. etc. etc.
Then another gentleman got up and gave a resumé (very
clearly done) of Comte's philosophy, and then Miss Peabody
(a Bostonian lady) refuted the Comte disciple with a Channing-
like sermon.[171]

In the evening we all met again and had a very delightful
evening. Mr. Spring read out loud for some time, then we
talked in knots together.

In this week there has been acting and music, etc. I have
been hard at work all day painting and have finished one big
picture. Doctor has been giving French lessons and taking
English lessons and fencing, or rather teaching the young men
for no one here can fence with him. I hope you will get (I send
it) *Antislavery Standard for May 1st*,[172] for there is something
about the Doctor there.

The weather is wet and cool with some days most beautifully
fine.

Doctor sends his kind regards to you all. He is better here,
though he looks very thin (as a limb).

We go to Mr. Neill's on Thursday 13th and on Saturday to
Boston, dear Pater. Ever your affect. Bar.

20 May.
Niagara.

My dearest Belos,

Thank you very much for the £14 which I accept to
spend partly in presents for the home people and partly for
myself.

Your drawings have been much admired. I wish I had more

of them. I should like to give presents to Mrs. Follen, Miss Cabot and others.

We kept yesterday by going over to British soil. We walked down to the beautiful suspension bridge which crosses the Niagara River about two miles below the Falls. They say here it is the only suspension bridge which carries a railway (not tubular) over on the Canada side. We were dressed up in oil-skin and went down behind the fall ('within the veil'). Only then does one at all feel the awful power of this fall of water. It is very grand, but the noise so deafening that a few minutes is as much as we could stand. The falls on this side are wider and you get a more extended view, but I like the American side much the best. Goat Island is so beautifully picturesque. The Canadians do not seem to like the Americans much, if we may judge by one day's experience. The Canadian ponies are very beautiful – a pair sells for £200 in America. The horses in America as a general rule are superior to the horses we see in England (I mean the mass – of course we have the best horses in the world and the best people, but the mass of people and of the horses in America are a happier looking set than ours in England – wretched ill-used donkeys, a few starving chickens – that is a comfort here). As a rule the Americans are kindly and use their animals and children as well.

Yesterday a boat and a man in it went over the falls. Some accident. Happier every year. We saw two beautiful wolves yesterday taken near here. My Doctor looked at them with profound affection. We are going to bring home a vieux hibou[173] which has fascinated us (not alive) and is a complete study to put in a picture. I shall bring home a great quantity of photographs which I have exchanged for pictures, much to my delight.

I wish it were not so cold. I have been drawing here, but it is very unpleasant and the icy wind from Canada cuts my face to pieces.

22 May.   Left Niagara at seven a.m., arrived at Toronto at twelve. Because along the shore of the Great Lake Ontario (which is just like the sea) we could not see the other side. People in the railway looked English: the girls with rosy cheeks and ugly features, some of the men of the Mister

Gratton type. We have a lovely day, cold but bright and blue. The trees here are just in bud, the corn a few inches up, the cherries out, but not the apples. 'God save the Queen,' 'Queen's birthday,' 'Excursions,' 'Proclamations' show us we are on British ground – also the absence of churches in Niagara. I saw ten or twelve and the population is only four thousand stationary (forty-five thousand visitors come during the summer and some of them, I suppose, go to churches). Here we walked near two miles and I did not see one church. With that exception I should not have known we were out of America. The white houses are just like the Americans'.

Among the One Thousand Islands on the St. Lawrence. This river is much more beautiful than the Mississippi. These islands are beautifully wooded and rocky like the islands on the Scotch lakes, only there are no mountains here to back them. I shall post all my letters at Montreal and let them go by the British mail this time. I hope dearest Belos, this will reach you in England and that you will be much better. There are two boats from Boston in June (16th and 30th). I do not know until I get my letters from home which we shall take. In two days I shall be in Boston. I want my Doctor to go to Quebec from Montreal for a few days and let me go to Boston alone. I don't want to go to Quebec – I have seen enough of Canada. I like it, but it is not so interesting to one as Boston. Best and devoted regards to you and Nanny from the Doctor with my love your affect. Bar.

I have never heard yet whether Aunty and Mr. Gratton have got into their new house. Give my best love to them. I could not find one new fern at Niagara for Mr. Gratton. We grabbed about everywhere to find one to send in a letter.

Sunday, 23 May.
Russell Hotel, Toronto.

My dear Pater,

Here we are in our gracious Queen's dominions, and very big dominions, too. After America Canada appears a desert without people. 40,000 here but the country between Niagara and here is not settled as on the other side and men go over there. As one said to Doctor, 'There is Canada – you have to pay church rates, and here none and better wages into the bargain.' The country we passed through yesterday was beautifully undulating with woods everywhere except where there were settlements. Here we are in a hotel full of M.P.'s, officers, divines and all the regular English respectabilities. They are terribly stupid after the Americans who have always something amusing and new to say, whether about the Mormons or California, or slavery, or their preachers or Shakers, etc. Here they talk about 'appointments,' 'places,' 'eldest sons,' 'Governor,' 'Bills,' etc.

In consequence of the piety of these people there are no boats, no trains going on Sunday, so we have been obliged to stay here and extremely stupid it has been. I went to five churches this morning! This afternoon we walked in the beautiful park in the rain. We have not seen a park in the United States to compare with this. I think the Americans hate trees.

> *Tuesday, 25 May.*
> *On board the 'Kingston' steamer.*
> *St. Lawrence River in the midst of the 1000 Islands.*

Yesterday we left Toronto in the morning with a crowd of Queen's birthday excursionists for Kingston. We were fortunate to have this opportunity of seeing the population enjoying themselves. The Canadians make a greater to-do than we do with the Queen's Birthday. The railway cars were very beautifully decorated with fir trees, flowers and flags. At some of the stations there were bands of music, and everywhere drinking and eating. None seemed to enjoy themselves so much as the French. One car was half filled with them. It is very curious to see how thoroughly French they are. They can speak English, but among themselves all speak French and such French! I can hardly understand it. Doctor says it is old French and he can understand them very well. Here on this boat there are families of Canadian French and they are very nice people, dressed in the English costume, hats and grey dresses – the most ladylike ladies I have seen and two very pretty with fine features and intelligent expressions. The French seem to be very happy and loyal subjects to the Queen and they are highly respected for their riches and because they are 'noble families.' They are all *obstinately national;* this may be said of the French everywhere. In the States they are the last to be assimilated (the Irish by the bye are the first. In the schools the children of Irish are hardly to be distinguished).

About the negro population we hear universally that they are doing well in a money sense, but as yet they have not taken an equal place with the whites and are not equally respected. For instance, white men rarely *marry* coloured women but white women of low class marry black men. The man who owned the principal omnibus at Kingston station was a coloured man and in the streets are met many, very well dressed.

The Catholics flourish in this part of the world and have new cathedrals in Toronto and Kingston (both very fine buildings) and many convents.

Wednesday, 26 May.
Montreal.

You are quite right, Pater. This is the most beautiful in America. Last night as we steamed up the river it looked lovely, the sun just setting behind it, lighting up the many spires and shining in the blue water in the foreground.

Coming through the rapids yesterday was quite exciting. When you were here the navigation of the rapids was thought impossible. Now the steamers let off all steam, take on board an Indian pilot and dash down between the rocks in a rough sea almost like the Atlantic waves. It looks dangerous but I believe it is not, as the channel (tho' only five feet wider than the vessel in some places) is well marked and the current takes the vessel all right.

I go to post this so Goodbye, yr. affect. Bar.

27 May.
Quebec.

Last night we found a boat starting for Quebec, so went to bed on board and woke up in the St. Lawrence this morning and very lovely it was. This is a *very* picturesque place the views of plain, river and hills surpass anything in the States I have seen.

We are in a French inn and see nothing but French. These people and the picturesque view remind me of some inns in

Montreal Wednesday 26th of May. You are
quite right Pater this is the most beautiful
in America. Last night as we steamed
up the river it looked lovely the sun just
setting home it lighting up the many ships

& shining in the blue
water in the foreground.
    Coming down the rapids yesterday was
quite exciting. When you were here the
navigation of the rapids was thought im...
now the steamers let off all steam take on
board an indian pilot & dash down between
the rocks in a rough sea almost like the
Atlantic waves it looks dangerous but
I believe it is not as the channel tho' only
5 feet wider than the vessel in some
places is well marked & the current
takes the vessel all right. yr aff M Bar-
    I go to port this so goodbye

Belgium. It is really artistique! Quite a treat to see this old town in this new world.

We fly to Boston and hope to hear good news.

We have been six days in Canada and seen an enormous deal of French, English, negroes, Indians, etc. etc.

Doctor enjoys this place. He says the moral level is higher here than in the United States, and he is right.

[Dr. Bodichon to Benjamin Leigh Smith].

27th May, 1858.
Quebec.

Dear Sir,

We have crossed the Canada from Hamilton to Quebec. There are striking differences between this country and the United States, physically and morally. At the great Republic are a strong activity, none or little appearance of government, many crimes against persons and property; every man is his own ruler for good or for evil. In the Canada a strong government appears by its policemen, soldiers, castles and various things of war. But there is less activity: we find more ragged boys and girls, small private houses and large public buildings (as, markets, churches, canals, courts of justice). The Canadians seem happier than the citizens of the U.S. The Frenchmen, above all, have kept their national gaiety: in the streets, steamboats, railroads, hotel, they are talkative fellows. They are much satisfied with the British government, and I believe that they are the most loyalist subjects of the Queen Victoria: prone in any way to resist against the invasions or amalgamations with the neighbour Republic. The Canada can become a great nation, but there is not yet time for it to remain without support of England. The emigration is not arrive here. The population increases by itself and not by foreigners. This prevents a rapid development and produces a stronger French and British element. Often the marriages bring forth ten or twelve children and now and then some centenaries are met.

Toronto, Kingston, Quebec and the country offer more physical variety than the towns and country of the United States. They can become a beloved place for the artist. Several Catholic priests with whom I have spoken said to me that the British government is very just for them. The different

ministers of religion habitually live friendly with each other. The Catholic and Anglican bishops exchange visits between them. If now, some furious cry *à bas le papisme*, they do not find adherents, and the Protestant ministers blame those cryers. In fact there is a complete harmony among the Protestants and Catholics. Barbara is well. Tomorrow or a day after we shall set off for Boston. I am respectfully your
Bodichon.

Friday, 28 May.
Quebec. Excursion to the Falls.

This morning was lovely – bright and blue, but a north wind biting and cold and no feeling of May in the air. In the picturesque little place opposite an old-fashioned French inn stand twenty-two little *calaches* or 'wagons' (as the Canadians call them when they speak English). We went out and surveyed them and picked out the one with the best of all the good little Canadian horses and got in. I do not suppose in many towns there exist nowadays such queer little things as these old-fashioned French *calaches*. To protect myself from the icy wind I put the cloth hood of my grey cloak over my head and to protect myself from the sun I put my broad-brimmed hat on the top of that. This costume is admirably adapted to the American climate and the only means of sitting out-of-doors to draw with impunity.

We rattled off through the picturesque town, over the wooden bridge in a northwesterly direction for the Falls, which are eight miles down below on the St. Lawrence where the Montmorency River falls from the hills into that great river. The country before was bare, not a tree in leaf, but looked cheerful because dotted over with white and grey houses whose roofs were made of metal plates and shone in the sun like silver. Beyond the houses the hills were covered with sturdy firs dark and thickly growing together, and beyond them rose the hazy blue mountains. The women we met (looking like French women, as they are) were very picturesque in short blue woollen petticoat, cotton jacket and big straw hat. Many were working in carefully kept gardens, others bring home the cattle. By the roadside we passed tall crucifixes and some little chapels exactly like those on the roadsides in Normandy. The houses have very sloping roofs built to shoot down the snow, and remind me of what I have never seen but in my mind's eye, the houses in Norway and Sweden. I am sure this country is exactly like Sweden.

We drove through some dark avenues of spruce fir and stopped at a lodge and got out and walked through a wood, guided by a roar fiercer (though not so loud) than Niagara. We went down some deep wooden ladders and stood close to the top of this tremendous fall. The black water was changed into one vast seething mass of tumbling foam two hundred and fifty feet long, and down below roaring in a whirlpool three hundred feet deep. Less than a year ago the suspension bridge which hung from the two piers standing above, though quite new – went down with a great crash and the poor people who were passing (two in a carriage and one on foot) went with it and were never seen again dead or alive.

We walked to the highest point which butted out above the St. Lawrence and had the finest view I have seen in America. The terrific falls of white foam against the black rocks and sombre firs, with deep blue mountain tops beyond and then the grand St. Lawrence which we looked up, with Quebec – a city of silver spires and silver domes glittering in the sun, the old grey fortifications crowning the hills, and the beautiful distances of hills – made one of the most singular and beautiful pictures I ever in my life saw.

The rocks and trees around the falls are very wild and savage, quite different from those near Niagara. I like these falls much the best. They are a hundred feet higher and though they are not unique of their kind, I like them best. I like the stern, gloomy country, the black mountain river changing into a pale ghost as it leaps the precipice.

The waters of Niagara are as green as the sea of the Atlantic and have not the appearance of a river at all. It is a beauty distinct and ought not to be thought of with anything else in the world. Montmorency is a real bit of mountain poetry to be found, thank God, in many lands.

Dear Pater,

Quebec is quite worth seeing. I did not want to see it. I was anxious to get to Boston but my Doctor said after your four letters telling us to see Canada, Montreal, and Quebec, it was not right not to go. I am heartily glad I went. Two days very well spent, because there is no more curious mixture than the French and English here and because the place is very picturesque.

The Doctor has enjoyed this Canada week very much. He finds friends everywhere in Quebec. He made friends with all sorts, from the Governor down to the cooks (newly imported immigrants). Until you travel in America you can have no idea of the extent of the tyranny in Europe. There are hundreds of Frenchmen, thousands I may say, who have left France, though not transported, because they could not bear the suspicions and petty vexations their opinions against Louis Napoleon expose them to. To live in constant fear of being arrested is too terrible to be endured, and we have met many who have come here to breathe freely.

My heart is ready to burst with indignation when I see how many lives this man has destroyed – how many good, clever men in mid-life who have had their whole prospect blighted by this tyrant. The Frenchman does not easily transplant himself and suffers always from homesickness *pour la belle France*.

You are right, it is a tyrant-ridden world. I wish Orsini had rid it of one tyrant.[174]

> *Sunday, 30 May.*
> *Pond Island, Vermont.*

Yesterday morning we crossed the ferry at Quebec and took our tickets for Boston, but found that the train stopped short here until over Sunday!! It seemed an infamous shame and we were disgusted, but being here in a lovely mountain country we are reconciled.

The journey yesterday was the most picturesque: wild fir woods by the side of the Richmond River, hills and blue mountains above them. The rocks are granite and the fir trees grow among them in wild confusion for miles and miles.

We had no trouble at the custom house whatever, and the Canadian French conductor took care of us and deposited us in this inn, where we find ourselves daintily served and have a fine view of lake and mountains.

We went for a walk round the lake, and as we passed round the foot of a little hill covered with fir trees we heard sweet voices singing a hymn in parts. This was evidently a little congregation gathered together to worship in their own way. I went into the only church and heard such a stupid man preach that I did not wonder at the dissenters.

The country which is cleared all about here is quite ugly – bare tree stems standing half-blackened with fire. The country which is not cleared is impassable from the mass of bramble and vines growing under the fire.

Monday, 31 May. Travelled all day through a beautiful country and saw the White Mountains covered with patches of snow, but I did not see one place where I wanted to stop because there is no walking except in the ugly places. As we neared Boston the country became alive like England – clean farms, lovely orchards in full blossom and delicious green meadows.

Tuesday, 1 June. Went to see Miss Clarke. Found in pretty rooms in the French style in a large hotel and her studio on the highest floor, five stories up. She was very kind and took us to these lodgings which are delightful, just what we want. The prettiest rooms we have had in America.

We spent the evening with her. Mr. Clarke was delightful and Mr. Freeman Clarke and the Doctor talked of religion, associations, Amalgamation.[175]

Wednesday, 2 June.[176] Went to British Exhibition: saw SOLD on two of my pictures!

Thursday, 3 June. I have met a large part of the best women today and like some of them very much. Doctor Harriet K. Hunt is perfect, charming and such a plucky little cove, the very pluckiest creature I ever saw.[177] I loved her. The women and she came to see me with flowers from the country and her hearty welcome of 'Oh, Barbara Smith, how do you do.' She has practised twenty years here and is much respected. She has the look of an English Quaker – solid.

The lady artists of Boston are going to give me a soirée next

Saturday. Ain't it funny! – Oh, that reminds me of the best joke of all: A gentleman who had heard of Barbara Smith as an artist went to see her pictures, not knowing I was married, did not understand the (Bodichon) which they had put, as well as BLS. 'Oh,' said a friend, 'it's the name of a style like P.R.B.,[178] you know, etc.' 'Oh, yes! ah!' So the gentleman goes to the clerk, and he wanting to be thought wise says, 'Oh, yes sir!' So the gentleman goes about saying, 'Barbara L. Smith is a fine artist, in the Bodichon style you know.' Miss Clarke hears of it and is in fits of laughter at the Bodichonite.

Dear Pater,
 Doctor sends his kind regards to you and all.
  With my love to Aunty and Mr. Gratton,
   Your affect. Bar.

Dearest Aunt Julia,
 Thanks for your two letters. I did not get them until 1st of June – both together. I shall be home on the 11th or 12th of July.

[*Circa 3–5 June. Boston.*]

My dearest Aunty and Mr. Gratton,
 I suppose you will not have my letters to Pater (as he is going to Algiers), so I write to tell you how very jolly I am. I have come home from the woods to the three doctors, for you must understand I went off to paint and my Doctor stayed here, coming down to see me by rail two or three times a week.

 I never was better in my life, though I hate the climate and the city. The people I like very much and like to see my pictures (thirteen of them) in the British Exhibition. I like, too, my painting room here and the uninterrupted time I have for painting. We breakfast at seven and I stay to work till two o'clock, then go out to see people and things.

 I wear your green ribbons in memory of you – have one on now. Why don't you write when one is far away? Letters are precious – you forget that – and though I am quite settled down here and feel at home, I always rush at the postman in a frantic state.

I never was happier in my life than here, but I would not live in America for £20,000 a year. I do not like it at all as a country to live in.

Dr. Bodichon sends you his kind regards and wishes you and Mr. Gratton all kinds of prosperity.

When we were in London he said he would rather go to see you and Mr. Gratton than any of the relations who only knew us lately, but he thought until he could speak it [English] it was a trouble to you. He says he feels the relations who were good to us as children are the only relations to be treated as relations.

Miss Cushman acts every night. I mean to go and see her as soon as this rain holds up. It pelts every day.

Your affect. Bar.

Friday, 4 June.
2 Boylston Place.

Saw Dr. Hunt again. She came with her bright-looking sister and Mrs. Sale, a Woman's Rights woman from Missouri with a noble but care-worn expression. They all three brought me emblematic nosegays.

Mr. Freeman Clarke came. Among other things he told me of the great admixture of employments in Maine, Vermont and Massachusetts. Many men labour at manufactories in winter and at outdoor work in summer. Along the coast numbers of men are shoe-makers all the winter and cod fishers all the summer in Labrador, etc.

Saturday, 5 June. Went to paint in Sara Clarke's studio. Mr. Stillmann came up with message from Lowell about meeting us. Stillmann is painting a picture for Lowell in a beautiful wood where we are to go.[179]

Dr. Bodichon went to the Museum and Library.[180] He will exchange lessons every day with a Dr. Reed here.

I went out to drive with Miss and Mrs. Clarke. We saw Mt. Auburn and then went to tea at Mr. Follarton. Came home; found Dr. had had Wendell Phillips,[181] Theodore Parker, Miss Barbara Channing, etc. etc., calling.

I saw Miss Peabody at Miss Clarke's. She is a dear one – a true mixture of Miss Jameson[182] and Aunt Julia.

I saw so much that interested yesterday and today that I feel quite exhausted with the number of new ideas.

Sunday, 6 June.   In the morning Theodore Parker.[183] In the evening at Dr. Howe's.[184] He has a fine face. Mrs. Howe pleasant. Miss Cushman there, as cordial as ever, looking splendidly well in spite of her tremendous hard work.

Monday, 7 June.   Many people and Emerson. He talked of Arthur Clough and his poem 'Amour de Voyage' which he used to defend, but now seeing the end, gives up.[185] He said the end was poor, bad, disappointing, an insult to readers. Reminded him of Tennyson's *Princess* in which event you are expecting something higher than the common end in darning stockings.

Mrs. Follen and Charles as kind and cheerful as ever.[186]

Went to Mrs. Cheney's art evening – pleasant to see a room full of casts and good things. I was very tired, so found it tiring, but there were ten or fifteen women all engaged in the study and practice of art and about as many men.

Tuesday, 8 June.   Nine o'clock. Went to Dr. H. K. Hunt. Glorious time with her. Mrs. Hall of Cambridge, a lady who graduated in the Central New York college, was there. She is wife to the Astronomer at the Observatory. We shall go and see her. She is a Woman's Rights woman.

Mrs. Severance, one of the best of the WRW,[187] came in and three other ladies. Dr. Hunt is like quicksilver and leads a capital life. She is more like a writer than any woman I have seen yet. I never saw such an active brain in my life. Theodore Parker said he did not like New York so well as Boston because he missed there his glorious phalanx of old maids.

I see there is a glorious band of old-maid workers here. One of them has a family of two hundred orphans whom she has adopted and arranged life for.

Mrs. Maria Chapman called.[188] She looks more beautiful than ever and was very cordial indeed to Dr. Suebius' friend.

Miss O'Sheen called (who knows all the old Breton families) and she and Dr. B. have endless talks of Brittany and its noble families, rich and poor. Curious to meet her here.

6 June.
2 Boylston Place, Boston.[189]

Went to the Music Hall to hear Theodore Parker preach – the vast hall was as full as it could hold below, and there were some hundred people in the two upper galleries – about –[190] in all.

The congregation was well dressed – but the most diverse I ever saw – before me sat a man dressed like a gentleman, but the black anchor on his brown hand told his profession; by him a merchant, beyond the merchant a brown young man without any shirt showing and gold earrings in his ears; behind me a sea of heads full of expression, men and women about equally mixed; some good heads. I saw a free lover and opposite a dark mysterious man and woman both with black spectacles on. They were, I think, Mr. and Mrs. A. T. Davis, Pough-keepsie seer and seeress.[191]

Mr. Parker sat in a chair behind the reading desk. He looks nearly sixty, is small and has very grey hair. His face and head are like Socrates and perhaps like St. Paul (I do not know St. Paul's face so well). He has a beautiful voice and when he began a noble thanksgiving for the beauties of this wonderful world he spoke like a poet and like a painter, describing the opening summer more like Ruskin than anyone else. – He had a glass of wild flowers which he clutched and used as an illustration. He prayed to the Creator, the infinite Mother of us all (always using Mother instead of Father in this prayer). It was the prayer of all I ever heard in my life which was the truest to my individual soul.

There was then some singing, a chapter of the Psalms of David, and then he came forward and gave an account of the meeting of *Progressive Friends* which he had attended in Pennsylvania. He said this was a yearly meeting of a body of men and women who had come out of the Society of Friends as we have come out from the Unitarian ranks.[192] There were three or four thousand present and all the farmhouses were open to take in the visitors who attended, and there were hundreds of carts and wagons full of labourers, farmers – fine big men – healthy wide women.

'I preached for them four times. – There were reports of the doings of the congregation for Emancipation, Rights of

Women, Temperance and Recreations for the People. It was a noble meeting and noble are the fruits of this society.'

He then preached a sermon on the ecclesiastical idea of God. It was the most remarkable sermon for force I ever heard in my life – He is indeed the noblest preacher in the world. No wonder thousands throng to hear him. And great credit to the thousands that they understand him. I find that the sermon is one I cannot take in part and give it. It was very learned, philosophical and logical. His comparison of religions was magnificent. He spoke of that mischievous faith in the saving power of Christ's blood, and said in as far as most other faiths put man on his own merits to be saved or banished, they were superior to Christianity.

He said Christian nations were not superior in morality to the Mahomedan, Buddhist and Zen – only vastly superior in intellect.

In his sermon he spoke strongly of Woman's Rights and of the evils of prostitution. His language was noble and strong, his manner of speaking grand. I was quite exhausted by the intense concentration of my faculties in history.

He spoke for one hour and five minutes. I had no idea how long he had spoken, whether it was half an hour or three hours. He looked to me more like an inspired man than any preacher I ever saw. It is worth while to come here to hear him.

June 8th. In the evening went with Dr. Sara Clarke and Miss Peabody (authoress of *Records of a School*) to Mrs. A. Lovell's at Cambridge. There we met James Lowell (poet), Dana (four years before the mast),[193] Professor Pierce, Mr. Sylvester's friend, Stillmann (artist), etc. etc. A very delightful evening – no fashionable stiffness, but easy manners and a pleasant atmosphere. I talked to Lowell, who said nothing remarkable but was very agreeable.

Miss Palfrey (daughter of that friend of Bessie, etc.) talks like a book.[194] I never heard anything like it before.

Cambridge is a delightful place and I like the people there. I see there are a few of the disadvantages of a village – everybody knows everybody there and there is a certain fear of everybody – so that ladies dare not wear hats if they wish it ever so much.

I went to see a medium in the afternoon with Miss Peabody.

Wednesday, 9 June.   Allston hunting (see list of his pictures).[195]

In the evening we went out into the country with Dr. Harriet Hunt to see her sister Mrs. Wright. Mr. Wright came to meet us at the cars and took us a pleasant drive and gave us some fine views of Boston harbour. We passed a delightful evening walking about the garden and hearing stories of Dr. Hunt's medical experience. She is one of the jolliest women I ever saw in my life. She makes me laugh more than anyone I have met in America. She gives a good account of the young women she says are growing up with right views and that the terrible ill health from which they suffer will be ameliorated by their knowledge of physiology. Mrs. Wright is a fine healthy woman, mother of four healthy boys and a girl.

Thursday, 10 June.   Painted. At three C. Follen came for us and we went out to see Mrs. Follen and Miss Cabot.[196] They live in an old-fashioned English house with a pleasant view of green fields and trees from their windows.

They have a nice garden and a better orchard – altogether a cosy, happy-looking place. Rooms large but low. Nothing could look happier than the three and we felt quite at home with them – as much so as if we had been in England.

Wendell Philipps came in the evening. He was enchanting. He told me that the W. R. Movement had made immense progress since 1850. He knows twenty women at least who can gain their living by lecturing in Lyceums. He says Lyceums in debt very often get women to come and lecture on W.R. even when they do not agree with her, because they know she will attract a paying audience. Gentlemen who were dead set against the W.R. now advocate it. A Governor of Ohio was obliged to apologize to the ladies of Ohio and recant because he refused to hear female delegates to some Society, etc. etc.

Wendell Philipps himself says when Lyceums come to him he says, 'Yes, I will lecture for you: 50 dollars for Literature or Abolition, or WR for nothing.'

He is a noble man – a man of genius who has sacrificed his ambition to his conscience. He has a clear, beaming expression and very agreeable manners.

He, like Emerson, has an invalid wife.[197]

I was delighted to hear all the proof of progress Philipps gave me. He says, 'We make more progress in the legislature than in society.' The reverse is true in England.

Friday, 11 June. At 11 a.m. S[arah] C[larke] and Dr. B. and I went to Concord to see Emerson. He lives in a quiet country house embowered in trees like a village gentleman's house. We had a most delightful and quiet time with him. I did not talk to him much. He talked to Dr. about French political writers, natural history, Africa, Paris, America. Not one word especially Emersonian was said by Emerson. He was very quiet and we sat on his doorsteps and enjoyed the garden and quiet idle sort of talk, S.C. and I sketching.

He looks 'tender and just' as S.C. said.

The weather has been so intensely hot that I feel utterly incapable of fully understanding all the ever-varying drama which moves so rapidly before me!

The heat is irritating here. In fact I think Boston climate very disagreeable.

12 June.
My dear Pater and all,

We are very well in spite of the great heat and horrid dust of this place – Boston has a detestable climate. But in spite of that it is a very interesting place and every day I see things and hear things which will be valuable to me for all my life.

I wish all the young men and women in England could come for a year of inspection here. It would do them a great deal of good. Some would stay because there is a much wider field here to choose a profession from. Some would go back with some new and valuable ideas.

I have not heard since the letter of 14 May saying they were coming home. I hope all is well. I send you my notes of what I have been seeing but it is only about half a record, as so many people come in while I am writing that I have hardly any time. It is impossible to say how very kind and pleasant these Boston people are. Miss S. Clarke is our best friend and she is friend to all the best people here.

She was a pupil of Allston and has painted some good pictures. One was bought by the Athenaeum here, others are in private galleries.

We went to see Miss Foley, a cameo cutter. She is very clever and ought to go to Rome to improve.

By the bye, it is worth recording that Longfellow (poet) bought Miss Steers' lovely little landscape,[198] and Marcus Spring the Cornfield by BLS.

Love to all,
yr. B.

1 'To be sent to Nanny when CW has copied it' [BSB's note in pencil].

2 William T. Haskell (1818–59) was a colonel, not a general as BSB (p. 57) says. He was educated at the University of Nashville (Tennessee), fought against the Seminole Indians in the war of 1836, admitted to the bar in 1838, member of the Tennessee House of Representatives 1840–1. He served in the Mexican War and in 1846 was appointed Colonel in the Tennessee Volunteers. He was elected as a Whig to the Thirtieth Congress (1847–9), and when BSB met him was apparently a practising lawyer. He died in an asylum in Hopkinville, Kentucky.

3 Georgetown Visitation Convent, founded in 1797–8 by the Sisters of the Visitation; its school was opened in 1799. It later established a 'poor school', the first free school in the District of Columbia.

4 Frederick Law Olmsted's classic observation of the South originally appeared in three parts under separate titles. BSB was probably reading *A Journey in the Seaboard Slave States, with Remarks on Their Economy*, first published in 1856. This was the portion most applicable to the Bodichons' journey.

5 BSB evidently means the asylum, not the House of Representatives.

6 Hickman, Kentucky, in 1858 a thriving post-village with five churches, a tin factory and an iron foundry.

7 Oberlin was the first college in the U.S. to admit Negroes (1835) and the first to give degrees to women (1844).

8 (1818–93). Lucy Stone supported herself at Oberlin by teaching and manual labour and graduated in 1847. She became a regular lecturer on the antislavery circuit and headed the call for the first American convention for Women's Rights. She married Henry Brown Blackwell in 1855 after he had promised to give his life to Women's Rights, but she never took his name.

9 'Women are generally more fixed to one place by their lives and could bring an element into legislation which would be very useful' *deleted from MS*.

10 Harriet Beecher Stowe's *Uncle Tom's Cabin*, 1852, has been called by Spiller, Thorpe and Canby's *Literary History of the United States*, the most influential novel in all history. Some of the significance claimed for it is surely hyperbolic (contrary to Charles

Sumner's belief, for instance, there probably would have been a Lincoln in the White House even if it had not been written), but its originality, in turning American fiction away from romance of an unreal past toward the more difficult and controversial present, is unmistakable, and its popularity unquestionable. In the first year it sold 300,000 copies in the U.S., and the forty publishers (legitimate and pirates) who issued it in England had a sale estimated at a million and a half copies. The *Spectator* announced an age of 'Tom-mania'.

11 In May 1856 Charles Sumner, a senator from Massachusetts, delivered an antislavery speech on the Kansas-Nebraska bill. Two days later he was assaulted and struck on the head by Preston S. Brooks, a representative from South Carolina. Sumner did not recover until 1859. BSB's phrase is probably from a Southern newspaper.

12 'Great questions of justice which every day live' *deleted*.

13 'In the one case we have the power of proving or disproving –in the other, not. Our moral responsibility is much greater in the first than in the second case' (BSB's note).

14 The sketch is not included in the MS. In July 1835 the citizens of Vicksburg, after professional gamblers had more or less taken over the town and defied its laws, seized a gambler named Cakler after a disturbance at a barbecue, took him to the woods and lynched him (in this case, without trial) whipped and tarred and feathered him and ordered him to leave town in forty-eight hours. The next night they lynched another in the same manner. When another gambler named North defied them they surrounded his house and when a citizen was shot and killed, the crowd rushed in, dragged out the inmates, without trial hanged five of them at the common gallows and left their bodies for twenty-four hours.

15 The leniency of the duelling law in either place is probably here exaggerated but the prosecution of the law was perhaps another matter. Mississippi punished any challenger, accepter, sender of challenge, second, aid, surgeon or person present advising and giving assistance at a duel with a fine of $300 to $1,000 and imprisonment of not less than six months and made them incapable of voting or holding civil or military office. It also held 'fighting in any village, town, or other public place' with 'rifle, shotgun, sword, sword-cane, pistol, dirk, bowie-knife, dirk-knife, or any other deadly weapon', or aiding such a fight, to be liable to the same penalty. When death resulted the participants were liable to the penalties for murder. The same penalties applied to persons leaving the state for the purpose of a duel. Louisiana was only slightly more lenient: death in a duel would entail the death-penalty for the victor and seconds, etc., would be liable as accessories before the fact. Challengers, seconds, agents or abettors would be fined no more than $200 and imprisoned not more than two years; accepters would be liable to a fine of $100 and a sentence of not more than one year. In November 1858 (just about a year after BSB writes) the Mississippi legislature passed an act for the relief of fifteen men 'for all acts heretofore committed in violation of any law of this state to prevent the evil practice of duelling', and were again made capable of holding office and voting, so that the prosecution of the law was perhaps less certain than its rather strict letter.

16 Not at all like a vetch's; it is an epiphytic bromeliad.

17 Kentucky's major port, on the Ohio River, which the Bodichons apparently visited before this diary begins.

18 MS. unclear: ?Jitney.

19 Neither Kentucky nor California was particularly more lenient in divorce legislation than the other states. Kentucky allowed separation from bed and board for any crime which was a cause of divorce *a vinculo* (such as cruelty or drunkenness) and allowed that 'when a husband annnounced in the papers his intention of not paying the debts of his wife, she has sufficient cause for divorce'. But in some respects Kentucky's law was more stringent than that of the other states: 'extreme cruelty' had to be continued for a period of six months or more to qualify as grounds for divorce. In a larger sense, of course, divorce in most states was 'easy' in comparison to divorce in England.

20 Founded by the French in 1717, New Orleans curves around the left bank of the Mississippi River, 100 miles from its mouth, protected from periodic flooding by a high embankment or 'levee'. In the 1850s it was the most important Southern port. In 1860 it had a population of more than 160,000, 35 churches, 40 schools, a university (U. of Louisiana) with medical and law schools, 20 newspapers (10 of which were dailies), 8 banks and 5 theatres.

21 Joseph Gratton (d. 1865), with whom BSB's aunt (on her mother's side, the 'Aunty' of this letter), Dorothy Longden, lived. At his death he left his residuary estate of £50,000 to her, 'now residing with me' (Gordon Haight, *George Eliot's Correspondence*, iii. 107).

22 In 1850 the federal government had made a great land grant to the railroads and stipulated how it would compensate the railroads for their necessary service in transporting the mails. Railroad aid then became railroad control: the earlier agreement (1838) that railroads would be compensated by a payment not to exceed 25 per cent above what 'similar transportation would cost in post coaches' was then revised. The complaints of bad service followed immediately: of 318 railway routes, 137 carried the mails without contract, 'departing and arriving at such hours and moving at such speed as was agreeable to them'.

23 A thick soup containing okra and chicken or seafood.

24 BSB's blank.

25 The Greeks called the statue of Amenophis III in Thebes, Memnon. BSB may be referring to this, or may simply be saying that the Negress looked Egyptian (see p. 83)

26 There was no single location for slave auctions in New Orleans. Sales were held generally at 'depots', hired for the occasion by the firms handling the sales, or at permanent addresses held by auction firms, such as J. A. Beard, which handled general and estate auctions as well. Neither this sale nor the one BSB attended on 13 February have been definitely located.

27 The First Congregational (Unitarian) Church, at the corner of St Charles and Julia Streets, a congregation which became Unitarian in the pastorate of Frederick Nott. The Rev. Mr Bolles was the current pastor, with services at 11 a.m. and 7 p.m.

28 A town to the west of New Orleans proper, made a part of the city in 1874. BSB calls it 'Carleton' in the MS., probably the way she heard it.

29 The University of Louisiana, probably on the medical school faculty.

30 That is, letters of introduction.

31 His name was apparently either Boylan or Izard and although BSB continues to refer to him as Chief or Colonel, it is more likely that he was a lieutenant (see 31 January 1858 and nn.).

32 The worst epidemic in the history of the city was in the summer of 1853: barrels of tar were burned on street corners and cannons fired to purify the atmosphere. On the worst day (in August) 230 deaths were reported. Total deaths from the fever were variously reported between 7,000 and 9,500.

33 North Carolina was the last state in the Union to eliminate significant property qualifications for suffrage, in 1850. Louisiana's state convention had eliminated them in 1845. There was universal white male suffrage (with some tests for literacy) by 1858 and in six states blacks were not excluded (Maine, New Hampshire, Massachusetts, New York, Rhode Island, Vermont).

34 Bessie Rayner Parkes (1829–1925), later Madame Belloc, mother of Hilaire Belloc. She had shared lessons with BSB, was a close friend, and introduced her to George Eliot. Buxton was the Bodichons' American agent.

35 BSB was too optimistic. The movement for Women's Rights in the U.S. dated from the World Antislavery Convention in London, 1840. Some delegates from that meeting organized the first Women's

Rights Convention, held in Seneca Falls, New York in 1848. The next significant meeting was a national convention in Philadelphia in 1854 and annual conventions continued until the Civil War and took up again following it, but progress in the state legislatures went little farther than resolutions and petitions. In 1867 the first serious legislative debates on the issue were held in New York and Michigan constitutional conventions, but the causes were lost (by a margin of only three votes in Michigan). By 1898 four Western states had given full voting rights to women (facilitated by the fact that they entered the Union under new constitutions) and by 1914, eleven states had given women the vote. The Nineteenth Amendment to the Constitution, passed in 1920, granted national woman suffrage.

36 Probably a kind of fireworks sold at this time of the year for traditional use at the celebration of Christmas.

37 The New Orleans, Jackson and Great Northern line: 'A passenger train leaves daily at 7:30 o'clock a.m. and arrives at Brookhaven, Miss., 128 miles from New Orleans at 2:25 o'clock . . . Fare, 3 cents each way' (advertisement in the *Picayune*).

38 BSB is drawing a distinction between the European *Cupressus* and the deciduous *Taxodium distichum*, the Southern or bald cypress, native to the U.S.

39 BSB put a blank in the MS. when she did not know the name or expected to insert it at a later time.

40 Apparently when registering as immigrants.

41 (1771–1845), journalist, clergyman and wit. He was a close friend of Julia Smith, BSB's aunt, and this is probably a story relayed by her.

42 Of *Uncle Tom's Cabin*, the daughter of unknown parents, who explained her existence as 'I 'spects I growd.'

43 Anna Mary Howitt.

44 Not so dated, but the entry seems to begin here.

45 An advertisement for this date in the New Orleans *Picayune*, for a succession sale by the State of Louisiana in succession of St Julien de Tournillon, Sr, includes a plantation, fifty-nine itemized slaves and, among other things, '45 pairs of chains'.

46 The collapse of Walker's expedition had dominated newspaper reports in New Orleans since 29 December. In 1855 William Walker (1824–60) landed an expedition of fifty-seven 'emigrants' in Nicaragua, whence he had been invited by the commander of a revolutionary faction badly in need of outside aid. With some help he captured Granada and ended the revolution, became the commander-in-chief of the army and virtual master of the state. In 1856 he was inaugurated President, but in 1857 made the mistake of seizing ships belonging to Cornelius Vanderbilt. He was soon deposed, and after attempts to regain the country was arrested and shot in 1860 by a firing squad in Honduras.

47 Probably a cue for a second newspaper clipping, perhaps an advertisement in the *Picayune* for the St Louis Institution in Dauphin Street, under the direction of Madam Déron: 'A beautiful garden surrounding makes the recreation literally a "path among flowers"; and all is so removed from the street as to give an air of retirement and tranquillity even in the midst of the city . . . Madam Déron in person constantly superintends the instruction, and always inculcates that dignified courtesy and modest and amiable manners, which, even more than letters, fit young ladies for the fulfilment of their duties in society. The feelings of regret and tenderness with which her many pupils now in "honored places" in the "world" still remember Alma Mater, speak the maternal kindness and firmness which govern her household.'

48 Lake Pontchartrain is a large (40 × 24 miles) lake about 5 miles north of New Orleans, accessible from New Orleans by canal at this time.

49 The *Picayune* carried a daily summary of 'Arrivals at the Principal Hotels Yesterday'.

50 The categories were social and customary rather than legal – any black blood was 'colour' in terms of the law, but three-quarters was called 'griffe', half was 'mulatto', one-fourth was 'quadroon', and one-eighth 'octoroon'. The fractional distinctions were perhaps more carefully drawn and attended in New Orleans, with its large free population, than elsewhere, and blacks there sometimes referred to themselves as 'Creoles de couleur'. 'Creole' had by this time lost its original definition of Spanish and French colonial descent and had come to mean simply nativeborn.

51 Probably the Mr Robinson BSB mentions on 26 December.

52 The Bodichons' American banker, Ezra Mill.

53 One of these advertisements: 'Mrs. Morrow, just from New York city, will tell the past, present, and future events of life. She is a seventh daughter, and has a natural gift, by invoking the powers of her wonderful science, so as to tell even the very thoughts. She is the most wonderful astrologist in the world, or that has ever been known . . . She has astonished thousands during her travels in Europe, and has been consulted by the most respectable ladies from all parts of the United States. All ladies that wish to consult her will do well to call soon, as she will remain in the city but a short time. Gentlemen not admitted . . . Fee $1' (the *Picayune*, 6 January).

54 A wide street parallel to the river between Nayades and Plaquemine.

55 BSB inserts this entry out of order so that she may finish her story, but she forgets and finishes the account of the twelfth before returning to the eleventh.

56 As of Emanuel Swedenborg (1688–1772). One of BSB's early schools was described as Swedenborgian.

57 Probably a cue for an enclosed newspaper clipping, untraced.

58 Misquoted from 'The Cry of the Human': 'And lips say, "God be pitiful",/Who ne'er said, "God be praised".'

59 The Lyceum, or local institution for popular education and public lectures, was held in City Hall.

60 Josiah Clark Nott (1804–73). The Library of Congress Catalogue lists *Instincts of Races*, 1866; *Physical History of the Jewish Race*, 1850; *Two Lectures on the Connection between Biblical and Physical History of Man*, 1848; and *Types of Mankind*, 1854, by Nott and *Indigenous Races of the Earth*, 1857, edited by him.

61 Several pages of the MS. seem to be missing here. Page size and the date on the verso place this leaf here. The account begins again in the midst of a description of BSB's young art student (see 9 January).

62 Mrs Elizabeth Cleghorn Gaskell's *Life of Charlotte Brontë*, 1857.

63 Elizabeth Jesser (1794–1866) married Dr John Reid. In 1847 she opened her house at 6 Grenville Street, Brunswick Square, for a course of lectures to women, and in 1849 took a house at 47 Bedford Square as a college for the higher education of women. Miss Frances Martin maintained a school in connection with this (1853–8). The college was later much enlarged to become Bedford College, incorporated in 1869.

64 'A young tornado with loss of life. At about two o'clock yesterday afternoon a young tornado burst upon the city, accompanied by rain which fell in torrents, doing, for the time it lasted, an immensity of damage. Ships and steamboats were torn from their moorings; signs, slates and awnings were hurled from their positions and sent waltzing through space; trees and horses were blown down, and in no less than three instances which have come to our knowledge the tornado was fatal to human life.' (The *Picayune*, 16 January. It goes on to list eight deaths.)

65 A small community on the west bank of the river immediately opposite the Vieux Carré.

66 'has been married three times: first husband she left in Europe' *deleted*.

67 'who cannot be called a lady' *deleted*.

68 A fine woollen stuff, generally grey or another subdued colour.

69 George Fox (1624–91), founder of the Society of Friends, refused to put off his hat to any, high or low. Vanaurburg has not been traced.

70 'I have not been able to resist the impression, that even where the economy, safety, and duty of some sort of religious education of slaves is conceded, so much caution, reservation, and restriction is felt to be necessary in their instruction, that the result in the majority of cases has been merely to furnish a delusive clothing of Christian forms and phrases to the original, vague superstition of the African savage' (Olmsted, *The Cotton Kingdom* (first published in 1856), 1953, p. 462).

71 See 11 May.

72 'The most daring and extraordinary feat ever attempted in the world by human beings will be performed by Messrs. Morat and Smith, at Place d'Armes (late Congo Square), on Sunday, January 24, 1858, being Mons. Morat's seventy-second, and Mr. S. S. Smith's fourth, and first ascension in this city.

'These gentlemen will make their terrific and unsurpassed Ascension on the bare backs of two monster Alligators (dispensing with the use of the car or other resting place).

'As novelty is the order of the day, this experiment will surely guarantee a full satisfaction to all in search of something new under the sun.

'After the inflation of the Balloon is completed, the two monstrous alligators (about 11 feet long each) will be harnessed in their paraphernalia (most beautifully and gorgeously caparisoned), in the presence of the spectators (affording much amusement), after which Messrs. M. and S. will take their departure from terra firma at the hour of 4 p.m. .... Admission 50 cents. Children and servants, 25 cents' (the *Picayune*, 23 January).

73 He is identified by the *Picayune* as the editor of the *Southern Citizen* of Nashville. The lecture was delivered before the Mercantile Library Association.

74 One of the gentlewomen whom BSB's father had brought into his household after the death of his wife to act as companion and perhaps governess for his children.

75 The chief reason this did not happen was the restrictions of new laws of 1831–50, passed after Nat Turner's rebellion, out of fear of a general slave rebellion and the fomenting power of literacy. In some states to teach blacks of any condition to write or read was illegal. There was a Presbyterian school in Charleston, South Carolina in 1740, a Quaker school in Virginia in 1785, a school in Charleston in 1810 run by freedmen and scattered 'play-schools' on plantations with the children of the owners teaching slave-children, but even these halting efforts were generally wiped out by the reaction to the threats of slave rebellion. The 'good New England women' did come in time: in 1862 Beaufort, South Carolina, was captured by Union forces and in an attempt to cope with the problem of now masterless slaves, schools were opened by the 'Yankee schoolmarms' of the American Missionary Association and the New York National Freedmen's Relief Association, even as the war continued just a few miles away. More followed in the wake of Reconstruction.

76 The allusion to Olmsted has not been traced; BSB may be confusing his with another traveller's account.

77 Possibly the St Charles Institute, in Greenville, a 'boarding school for young ladies conducted by M'me. C. Mace' (the *Picayune*, 23 January).

78 Spofford was justice of the Supreme Court of Louisiana.

79 Isaac Osgood and his wife Jane Rebecca Hull Osgood were of New England ancestry and had developed 'Magnolia' plantation in Plaquemines Parish (the S.E. extremity of Louisiana, bisected by the mouth of the Mississippi). They later became dissatisfied with slavery and moved north.

80 A first cousin: Florence Nightingale's mother Frances Smith and BSB's father Benjamin Smith were both children of William Smith (1756–1835).

81 This and the preceding word are uncertain readings of the MS.

82 The Howard Association of London was devoted to prison reform. The Young Men's Howard Society of New Orleans seems to have been concerned with nursing as well. It was staffed chiefly by clerks (according to a contemporary account) and depended on private contributions for cash support.

83 By M. Chénal, 'one of his unique concerts on the Russian piano and the magic cane . . . with other instrumental music' (the *Picayune*, 28 January).

84 *Charles VI* by Jacques François Fromentale Elias Halévy, at the Orleans Theatre.

85 That is, trash discarded here, or rejects dumped here.

86 'Large Larceny. – J. Hagg was last night arrested by special officers Boylan and Izard, on a charge of having stolen from Mr. T. L. Jones a valise containing $100,000 of notes and bills. The larceny is alleged to have been committed about a year ago in the Iron House on Tchoupitoulas Street. It is said that the accused had been attempting to negotiate the sale of the stolen papers' (the *Picayune*, 30 January). This would seem to indicate that BSB's friend was not a chief or colonel of police, but only a lieutenant.

87 Not traced.

88 BSB uses the short title employed in the book as running title: properly it is *A Journey in the Seaboard Slave States with Remarks on Their Economy*, 1856. The conversation she alludes to is between two drovers, one telling the other about his dream of hell (*The Cotton Kingdom*, ed. Schlesinger, 1953, pp. 278–9).

89 A custom which dated to the early nineteenth century. A cannon was fired at 8 or 9 p.m. to warn those who were out without permission to return to their homes and sailors to return to their ships. A pass issued by a merchant or employer was required of everyone found on the streets after curfew, and most of the taverns and shops closed their doors then.

90 A popular nineteenth-century concept of the paganism of black tribes.

91 Probably the area between Constance Street and the river from St Joseph Street to Louisiana Avenue, also called the 'Irish Channel', and already by this time long known as a trouble spot.

92 The New Orleans Workhouse, located on Perilliat Street, was at this time leased to a private operator, to whom the city allowed $11,000 per annum for expenses, which was less than it had cost the city itself to operate the institution.

93 Probably either James (1785–1855), or Francis Surget (locally pronounced 'Suzette', and probably spelled phonetically by BSB), brothers who owned plantations in Adams County and Natchez, Mississippi. Of the two, Francis Surget owned more slaves (367 according to one tax roll), but the number of 1,000 was probably an atrocity-story variation (information obtained from Laura D. S. Harrell of the Mississippi Department of Archives and History in Jackson).

94 An appropriation of the U.S. Congress had provided a station in Africa for the return of smuggled slaves taken by revenue officers in 1819 and the new colony had been further supported by the American Colonization Society with money and transportation for freed slaves. The colony was struggling and sometimes fighting outright with the indigenous population in the early years, but by this time, far from 'failure', had succeeded in asserting its claims as an independent republic. BSB may simply mean that sending slaves back to Africa does not solve the problem of slavery.

95 Not located.

96 Amelia M. Murray (1785–1884), *Letters from the United States, Cuba and Canada* (New York, 1856); Fredrika Bremer (1801–65), *Homes of the New World*, tr. by Mary Howitt, 2 vols (New York, 1853); James Stirling (1805–83), *Letters from the Slave States* (London, 1857); Sir Charles Lyell (1797–1875), *Travels in North America* (London, 1845) and *A Second Visit to the United States . . .* (London, 1849); and Charles Dickens (1812–70), *American Notes for General Circulation* (London, 1842).

97 The Parish Prison and Police Jail was located in a square bounded by Orleans, St Ann, Treme and Marais Streets. No evidence has been located that either it or the Workhouse (see p. 97 and n. 92) made available the kind of unofficial punishment BSB suggests.

98 (1802–87), English philanthropist and writer on education and reform. She founded reformatories and worked for the rescue of juvenile criminals.

99 In 1852 manumission was allowed only if the slave left the country thereafter, in 1857 a short and direct statute was enacted, 'that from and after the passage of this act no slave shall be emancipated in this state'.

100 For a number of years a moneymaking attraction. Painted by Rembrandt Peale (1778–1860), it measured 24 by 13 feet, and was first exhibited in his gallery at Baltimore. It was displayed in New Orleans at Armory Hall, beginning on 10 February (the attraction which had preceded it in town was Rosa Bonheur's 'The Horse Fair'). According to the advertisement in the *Picayune*, it was owned by the Peale family, and had 'never been valued at less than twenty-thousand dollars . . . It teaches the uncertainty of life, the certainty of death, the evils of war, the dangers of worldly pleasure, the results of intemperance, and the triumphs of religious faith over death. The great moral lesson it conveys to the beholder will live with him through life . . . Tickets 25 cents.' The painting is now in the Detroit (Michigan) Institute of Arts, a gift of George H. Scripps in 1885.

101 William Henry Hunt (1790–1864) instructed BSB in painting in her youth.

102 A maker or seller of images or statuettes.

103 'The buying and selling operation is certainly very unpleasant and revolting to our ideas, and the whites here dislike it; but it is curious how very little is thought of the matter by the blacks themselves. It is not true that women can be sold away from their children; but slaves often urge their masters and mistresses to sell them for some fancy or freak, and a gentleman to-day had a quarrel with his negroes, because he wanted to set them free . . . With all my love of liberty, if I was of the black race, I should much prefer being a slave upon one of the Southern plantations than any free black man or woman I ever met with in America' (Amelia M. Murray, *Letters from the United States, Cuba and Canada*, 1856, p. 274).

104 Probably John Kenrick (1788–1877), Unitarian and classical scholar, tutor at York and later professor of history at Manchester New College (which became Manchester College in 1893).

105 Mobile, the chief port of Alabama and after New Orleans the nation's greatest cotton market, was thirty miles north of the Gulf of

Mexico on the west bank of the Mobile River just north of Mobile
Bay (site of Farragut's 1864 naval victory, its mines the occasion of
his 'Damn the Torpedoes, Full Speed Ahead!'). Its population in
1860 was 29,258 and it had a theatre, three banks and six newspapers.
Roper House is listed in the 1856 and 1859 city directories in St
Louis St, between St Joseph and Royal – Mrs C. M. Roper, pro-
prietress, and B. F. Roper, clerk. The establishment seems to have
continued through the war and is last recorded in 1875 (information
supplied by Mrs John F. Lyle of the Historic Mobile Preservation
Society).

106 There was *some* drainage, of course, and the city fathers were
hard at work attempting to improve it (the budget for 1856–7 was
more than $26,000). Nevertheless, 'Much litigation has been the
consequence of the defects of the system', and Mayor C. M. Water-
man, in his message to the Common Council of New Orleans for
1857, anticipated much more expense 'caused by the inefficient
working of the machines now in use'.

107 Founded by Bishop Michael Portier in 1829 as a college and
seminary, it was by this time being run by the Jesuits. In 1860 it is
proudly listed as having a library of 7,000 volumes. It is now (as of
1962) a small four-year co-educational liberal arts college.

108 Daughter of the Mayor of Mobile and the descendant of a
Signer of the Declaration, Octavia Walton (1810–77) married Dr
Henry LeVert and was indeed '*the* Lady of the South'. No visit to the
South was apparently complete without some glimpse of her and
her tours of the North and Europe were little short of triumphal
progresses: Thomas Sully painted her portrait, Washington Irving
declared that a century produced only one such woman, Henry Clay
remarked upon the grace of her tongue, Lafayette praised her and
Queen Victoria sent her an invitation without a prior introduction.
She was variously designated 'Belle of the Union', 'Magnolia
Flower of the South', and 'Sweet Rose of Florida' (where her father
was territorial secretary for a time and where she was apparently
responsible for naming the new capital of Tallahassee). She had at
this time just returned from the Mardi Gras season in New Orleans.

109 George Henry Lewes's *Biographical History of Philosophy*,
1845–6, and Mrs Gaskell's *Life of Charlotte Brontë*, 1857.

110 Not traced.

111 Montgomery, Alabama, was the state's leading centre of cotton
production and a junction of the Montgomery and West Point
Railroad. The population in 1850 was 35,904, of which 23,710 were
slaves.

112 *Remarks on Prisons and Prison Discipline in the United States*
(Boston, 1845) and her various 'Memorials' to the legislatures of

Massachusetts, Tennessee, Kentucky, North Carolina, Mississippi, Pennsylvania and Maryland (1843–52). Dorothea Lynde Dix (1802–87) devoted her life to prison reform.

113 General Ignacio Commonfort (1812–63), a Creole, had been minister of war in the Alvarez cabinet when Juarez was minister of justice. The liberals and moderates asked Alvarez to give up the presidency to Commonfort, which he did in December 1855. He was elected President in 1857, but failing to support the liberal proposals for the constitution and defeated by lack of congressional support, he resigned the presidency and took flight to the U.S. 21 January 1858 and thence to France. The story of the *coup* (even as the story of Walker's defeat in Nicaragua) had received heavy coverage in New Orleans newspapers.

114 BSB is mistaken: it was precisely his lack of support for liberal measures to reform the constitution and curb the church which forced his resignation.

115 Thackeray visited the States in 1852–3 and 1855–6, but insisted, in the midst of the flurry of travel-books and American diaries, that he would *not* write a book on America, and he kept his word. Charles Mackay (1814–89), *Life and Liberty in America; or Sketches of a Tour in the United States and Canada*, 1859; Alexander Mackay (1806–52), *The Western World; or Travels in the United States n 1846–7*, 1849.

116 A note in the MS. here reads 'Quot. that', evidence that BSB was perhaps at one point thinking of publishing the diary *in toto*.

> Fama, malum qua non aliud velocius ullum,
> Mobilitate viget virisque adquiret eundo;
> Parva metu primo, mox sese attollit in auras
> Ingrediturque solo et caput inter nubila condit.

(For Rumor of all evils the most swift. Speed lends her strength, and she wins vigour as she goes; small at first through fear, soon she mounts up to heaven, and walks the ground with head hidden in the clouds. *Aeneid* iv. 174–7.)

117 Savannah, Georgia, 18 miles inland on the right bank of the Savannah River, boasted sixteen churches and a synagogue, six banks, a historical society and a public library of 'near 6,000 volumes'. Founded by James Oglethorpe in 1732 as the first settlement of his colony of debtors from English prisons and persecuted Austrian protestants, it fell to the British in the Revolution in 1778 for a time; BSB's hotel is named for Gen. Kasimierz Pulaski, who fell defending the city from a second British attack. BSB's great grandfather and great uncle, at some cost to the family fortunes, sacrificed their legal claims to a large part of this city out of sympathy with the Colonists during the Revolution. In 1860 Savannah had a population of

22,292, 7,710 of which were slaves.

118 Not traced.

119 Probably a cue for a clipping, now missing.

120 Daniel Webster (1782–1852), congressman and senator and Secretary of State under three presidents, unsuccessful Whig candidate for President in 1836; most notable as a staunch defender of the Constitution and as a brilliant orator. The quotation is from his second speech on Foote's resolution, 26 January 1830.

121 Henry Wadsworth Longfellow (1807–82), 'The Slave Singing at Midnight', in *Poems on Slavery*, 1842.

122 Isabella, BSB's sister.

123 Perhaps connected with the reference BSB makes to posters for grizzly bears, see above, end of entry for 28 February.

124 The marriage of the Princess Royal to Prince Frederick William of Prussia, 25 January 1858.

125 John James Audubon (1785–1851), artist of the great *Birds of America* (1827–38).

126 She had been ill in the autumn of 1856 with consumptive symptoms.

127 Dr Elizabeth Blackwell (1821–1910), the first woman doctor of medicine in modern times. She was born in Bristol and studied at Geneva, New York, and at La Maternité in Paris. She was the author of *Pioneer Work in Opening the Medical Profession to Women*.

128 Augusta, Georgia (pop. in 1860, 12,493), was reached by steamer up the Savannah; Wilmington, North Carolina (pop. in 1860 9,552) was a junction for the Wilmington and Raleigh Railroad north to Weldon, North Carolina.

129 Possibly at the opening of the Great Exhibition, 1 June 1851 but more likely on one of the Queen's many subsequent visits to the Crystal Palace before the Exhibition closed.

130 That is, turpentine and resin from the long-leaf, loblolly or 'slash' pines.

131 Of the American Revolution.

132 'But the great mass, as they are seen at work, under overseers, in the fields, appear very dull, idiotic, and brute-like; and it requires an effort to appreciate that they are, very much more than the beasts they drive, our brethren – a part of ourselves' (Olmsted, *The Cotton Kingdom*, 1853, p. 32).

133 The head of steamboat navigation for the Roanoke River; four railroads met here.

134 The capital of Virginia; in 1860, pop. 37,910 (11,699 of which were slaves and 2,576 freed blacks). The rapids are the lower falls of the James River.

135 Aquia Creek feeds into the Potomac north of Fredericksburg.

136 Buildings occupied by a Phalanx, or its community.

137 William George Spencer Cavendish, 6th Duke of Devonshire, died 18 January 1858.

138 A travelling exhibition of British artists organized for a tour of America. There were apparently 167 oils and 175 watercolors

139 Probably James Joseph Sylvester (1814–97), mathematician. He taught at the University of Virginia 1841–5 and later at Johns Hopkins and Oxford. Joseph Henry (1797–1878) was the designer of an improved electromagnet, a professor of the College of New Jersey at Princeton, and the first secretary and director of the Smithsonian Institution.

140 Part of the MS. has been torn away.

141 Rembrandt Peale painted Washington in 1795 when he was just seventeen, as he was sitting to a portrait by his father, Charles Willson Peale. He later worked to perfect an ideal portrait of Washington by combining elements from his and his father's portraits.

142 Gamaliel Bailey, M.D. (1807–59), the Cincinnatti (Ohio) philanthropist whom the American and Foreign Antislavery Society chose, together with J. G. Birney (see 11 May), to edit the *National Era*, a weekly to which John Greenleaf Whittier and Nathaniel Hawthorne contributed and in which *Uncle Tom's Cabin* was serialized. He and his paper had become a centre of political and social discussion in Washington. Bailey's house was a meeting-place for the Free-Soil Party.

143 Peter Parker (1804–88) was the first Protestant medical missionary to China. He organized the Medical Missionary Society of China in 1838, and in 1844 helped to negotiate the first United States treaty with China. He was American Commissioner and Minister to China 1855–7.

144 Part of verso of MS. torn away.

145 He really wasn't, but his claim was an elaborate one. Alexander Humphrys-Alexander, soi-disant Earl of Stirling (1783–1859) claimed the title under an alleged charter of *Novodamus* of 1639 which held that the peerage would go to the eldest heir female of the last of the heirs male, failing further heirs male. He claimed possessions of that Earl in Nova Scotia in 1831 as 'Hereditary Lieutenant and Lord Proprietor of the Province of Nova Scotia and the Lordship of Canada' and offered a million acres of New Brunswick for sale, shortly thereafter created a friend and adviser a Baronet of Nova Scotia. In 1839 he was indicted for forgery and the charter on which he based his claims was unanimously pronounced forged (apparently executed by Mlle. Le Normand, Parisian fortune-teller and friend of his wife) but it was held not proven that he had done the forging. His sons after him undertook further claims (GEC *Complete Peerage*, XII, appendix G, pp. 16–17).

146 A fine architectural achievement is probably what BSB means: the building of the Department of the Interior was designed by Robert Mills, completed in 1849, and a contemporary gazeteer describes it as 'not surpassed by any structure in Washington for extent or elegance, if we except the Capitol'. Lincoln's Second Inaugural Ball was held there and it has recently been restored, half housing the National Portrait Gallery and the other half the National Collection of Fine Arts (under the Smithsonian Institution).

147 In addition to the £300 per year Benjamin Smith had settled upon BSB at her majority, he seems also to have helped out in paying for her European trip and her trip to Algeria (in the autumn of 1855; see Biographical Introduction).

148 See 11 May.

149 The owner, John A. Washington, Jr. (a great-great-nephew of George Washington), finally (6 April 1858) sold the estate to the Mount Vernon Ladies' Association of the Union, chartered by the Virginia Legislature and founded by Ann Pamela Cunningham, for $200,000 raised by public subscription.

150 Public levees for formal calling were instituted by George Washington in order to regularize desirable formalities. His levees were rather cold and regal, but John Adams had only puritan disapproval of the third President's availability: 'Jefferson's whole eight years was a levee'. The practice continued into the Grant administration and thereafter survived as 'receptions' of a slightly different sort. Harriet Lane, President James Buchanan's orphan niece, served as the bachelor president's hostess during his term in the White House.

151 Charles Mason and Jeremiah Dixon, two English surveyors, surveyed, 1763–9, the disputed boundary between Maryland and Pennsylvania. The line, meant to serve as the northern boundary of Maryland, Delaware, and the part of Virginia which became West Virginia, came popularly to be considered the boundary between Free and Slave States, a symbolic division between North and South.

152 Left blank by BSB.

153 Mrs Jane Grey Cannon Swishelm (1815–84), active in Women's Rights and antislavery movements, married to James Swishelm, a farmer. In 1847 she established the *Pittsburgh Saturday Visiter*, which supported abolition and Women's Rights and in 1850 published an attack on Daniel Webster's private life (his tendency to compromise made him unpopular with the abolitionists). In 1857 she was divorced by her husband on grounds of desertion, and moved to Minnesota to start newspapers in St Cloud. She was Mrs Lincoln's friend.

154 William Henry Furness, Unitarian minister of Philadelphia and associate of Lucretia Mott. He spoke at the funerals of both James and Lucretia Mott.

155 Thomas Mott.

156 Theodore Parker (1810–60), in *A Discourse of Matters Pertaining to Religion* (1842), had seen Christianity as the highest ascent of the universe, the direct exposure of humans to divine reality, and he demanded a new theology to correspond with this view. In June 1845 he was installed as the minister of the Twenty-Eighth Congregational Society of Boston, meeting in Music Hall. He was a violent abolitionist, at one time advocating the rescue of a fugitive slave by an attack on a courthouse, and at another, meeting with John Brown (4 March 1858) for a project which involved a foray into the Virginia Mountains.

157 A small farm called 'Roadside', about 8 miles out of town on the old York Road, to which they had moved in 1857. Lucretia Mott (1793–1880) was a Quaker, reformer, abolitionist and much sought-after speaker for liberal causes. She had been a delegate to the World Antislavery Convention in London in 1840.

158 A four-wheeled carriage, open at the sides, with two or three seats and a standing top.

159 Anne Isabella Milbanke had been involved with Lucretia Mott in the controversy surrounding Harriet Beecher Stowe's article in the *Atlantic Monthly* about her. Elizabeth Reid was the founder of Bedford College, in which BSB and Julia Smith had enrolled in 1849 (see 14 January).

160 Bessie Rayner Parkes (see 27 December 1857).

161 Probably Mary Howitt.

162 The Raritan Bay Union was a semi-communal community, the spiritual descendant of Brook Farm and the North American Phalanx, a product of that time when, as Emerson remarked, everyone was 'a little wild . . . with numberless projects of social reform; not a reading man but has a draft of a new community in his waistcoat pocket'. But R.B.U. was more notable in its personnel, its longevity and its pioneering accomplishments than this implies. Marcus Spring founded it in 1853 when he broke off from the North American Phalanx (1842- *ca.*1854) in a disagreement about the function of religion and morality in the community, wishing to form a group which might find an intermediate position somewhere between the Phalanx and ordinary society. R.B.U. was to be less of a commune and perhaps less of a community. Each family had a private suite in a large hotel-like structure Spring built, some had private dining-rooms, there was sharing of work and the same system of pay as in the Phalanx ('Every man will be paid for what he does and no man will be paid for nothing'). One member, reporting her day, said, 'I didn't like to hear how many cents worth everything I ate was, but I think likely it is a good way when one gets used to it'. Lots could be purchased for construction of independent dwellings, with the central building containing 'the various common or general labours of the place such as washing, baking, storage, education and mechanical operations'. The advantages to residents were economies of cost and labour through central purchasing and sale at cost to consumers, and through communal sharing of services. The preamble to the R.B.U. constitution spelled this out more idealistically: 'To establish branches of agriculture and mechanics whereby industry, education and social life may in principle and practice be arranged in conformity to the Christian religion and where all ties conjugal, parental, filial, fraternal and communal which are sanctified by the will of God, the laws of nature and the highest experience of mankind, may be purified and perfected; where the advantages of co-operation may be secured and the evils of competition avoided by such methods of joint stock association as shall commend themselves to enlightened conscience and common sense.' It was capitalized at $500,000 and began business with $6,000, selling shares at $240 each.

What distinguished it from both Brook Farm and the North American Phalanx was its child-orientation and concentration on education: 'the central idea was a school where bodies, minds, hearts and souls should be trained to noble uses'. It pioneered in co-education and was the first school in America in which young women were 'educating their limbs in the gymnasium'. The school attracted students from as far away as California, but as Mrs Spring said later, 'Perth Amboy never knew how good it was'. The Eastern Intellectual Establishment did know, though, and the community was visited by Horace Greeley, George Inness, Louis Comfort Tiffany, Bronson Alcott, William Cullen Bryant, Gerrit Smith, Emerson and Thoreau. Emerson lectured there ('I could go to Mr. Spring's . . . my price abroad is $50, but I suppose $30 would do at Eagleswood') and Thoreau came for a brief visit: 'There sat Mrs. Weld . . . and her sister, two elderly gray-headed ladies, the former in extreme Bloomer costume, which is what you may call remarkable; . . . James G. Birney, formerly candidate for the presidency . . . Edward Palmer, the anti-money man (for whom communities were made) . . . Some of them, I suspect, are very worthy people. Of course you are wondering to what extent all these make one family and to what extent twenty ... The hardest thing to find here is solitude – and Concord.' And again, as with Brook Farm, this perhaps was the trouble in paradise. William Ellery Channing warned of this sort of thing early on: 'As I look over Brook Farm and North American Phalanx life I cannot but feel anxious as regards this new germ of the R.B.U. which we are planting with blind confidence that it is a seed from the Tree of Life, are you sure, then, that it is not an ill seed and apple of discord?'

Mr Spring purchased back all the stock in 1858 or 1859, the Springs departed in 1860–1 because of their son's illness, and the R.B.U. became the Eagleswood Military Academy and later the Eagleswood Park Hotel. Mrs Spring wrote in 1885: 'Poor dear Eagleswood, "that sacred spot," ... How we planted and built, and spent money there! A noble company gathered there ... And now I sit alone on the grave of great hopes. I look back and see a light that went out from it – small, but bright and pure and true' (Maud Honeyman Greene, 'Raritan Bay Union ...', *Proceedings of the New Jersey Historical Association*, LXVIII, no. 1, January 1950, pp. 1–19; Morris Schonbach, *Radicals and Visionaries: A History of Dissent in New Jersey*, Princeton, Van Nostrand, 1964, pp. 42–4).

163 Theodore D. Weld, an abolitionist, and his wife Angelina (Grimke) Weld had been brought in to work in the school.

164 Marcus Spring (1810–74) married Rebecca Gould Buffum (*ca.* 1811–1911) in 1836. They had travelled extensively and visited in reform and abolitionist circles in England, which accounts for the Smiths' previous acquaintance.

165 Zeus's cup-bearer on Olympus.

166 Eventually not only Mr Birney but Lydia Buffum Arnold (Mrs Spring's sister), Nathaniel Peabody (Elizabeth Peabody's father) and two of John Brown's associates in the Harper's Ferry Raid, Absolom C. Haslett and Aaron Dwight Stevens, were buried here; the latter had expressed a desire to Mrs Spring that they be buried in Northern soil.

167 James Gillespie Birney (1792–1857), a former slave-owner and representative in the Alabama legislature, had become an abolitionist and formed the Kentucky Antislavery Society. He was a leader in that faction of the movement which sought abolition by political as well as by moral persuasion. He was nominated for the presidency of the United States by the Liberty Party (an antislavery convention) and polled 7,069 votes in 1840. He was one of the vice-presidents for the World Antislavery Convention in London the same year. He ran again for president in 1843 and polled a popular vote of 62,300. He died as the result of a fall from a horse in November 1857.

168 Gerrit Smith (1797–1874) had tried to colonize blacks in the Adirondack wilderness and failed. He took on a number of other causes – Women's Rights, temperance, anti-tobacco, vegetarianism, Sunday observance, prison reform, abolition of capital punishment. He was again active in antislavery in the New England Emigrant Aid Company and in the Kansas Aid Society. In February 1858 John Brown was at Smith's home in Peterboro, New York, to obtain his help and financial support. He apparently was accessory before the fact to the raid on Harper's Ferry. He was later a member of Congress.

169 Eliza Woodson Burham Farnham (1815–64) was Matron of Sing Sing Prison 1844–8. She organized a society to take New York girls west, endorsed by Horace Greeley and Henry Ward Beecher. In 1856–8 she studied medicine, but returned later to her work in re-locating women, leading several parties of women west.

170 Arnold Buffum (1782–1859), Mrs Spring's father, a Quaker, was an active antislavery lecturer, the president of the New England Antislavery Society and the founder of the American Antislavery Society of Philadelphia.

171 Elizabeth Palmer Peabody (1804–94) opened a private school in Boston, became Bronson Alcott's assistant at Temple School in Boston (about which she wrote the book BSB refers to, properly titled *Record of a School*, 1835). She introduced Nathaniel Hawthorne to her youngest sister, who became his wife (another sister married Horace Mann). She published at her own press three of Hawthorne's works and Margaret Fuller's translations and *The Dial*. She established the first American kindergarten in 1860. For Channing, see p. 181, n. 162.

172 The organ of the New York Antislavery Society (1840–72); the clipping is not traced.

173 Old owl, apparently stuffed.

174 Felice Orsini (1819–58) had lectured in England. In 1857 he went to Paris to assassinate Napoleon III because he was an obstacle to the revolution in Italy. On 14 January 1858 he threw bombs under Napoleon's carriage, killing ten and wounding one hundred and fifty-six. He was guillotined on 13 March.

175 James Freeman Clarke (1810–88) was the founder in 1841 of the Church of the Disciples in Boston (Unitarian), a pioneer in calling forth the power of the laity in church affairs, and active in temperance, antislavery and Women's Rights. His older sister Sara Ann (1808–after 1888) was a landscape painter, exhibiting at the Boston Athenaeum and the American Art Union.

176 Dates for 1, 2, 3 June were mistakenly written 2, 3, 4 June.

177 Dr Harriet Kezia Hunt (1805–75) was a self-taught physician. She had been refused admittance to the Harvard Medical School in 1847 and again in 1850. She was active in antislavery and Women's Rights.

178 For Pre-Raphaelite Brotherhood, signed after or instead of a signature by member artists in some instances.

179 James Russell Lowell (1819–91), poet, at this point professor of modern languages and literature at Harvard and editor of the *Atlantic Monthly*; William James Stillman (1828–1901) studied with Frederick Edwin Church and was a friend of Ruskin's. In 1855 he founded a journal, *Crayon*, and moved to Cambridge in 1856. Shortly thereafter he gave up painting almost entirely and took up art criticism.

180 Probably the Harvard Medical School, in Boston at this time.

181 Wendell Phillips (1811–84) had made his name in antislavery circles with a speech protesting the murder of Elijah P. Lovejoy, an antislavery editor killed in 1837 defending his presses from a mob. He, too, had been a delegate to the World Antislavery Convention where he supported Women's Rights on the floor, leading to the seating of Lucretia Mott and other women previously excluded. He believed that the U.S. Constitution was a compromise with pro-slavery powers.

182 Anna Brownell Jameson (1794–1860), BSB's friend, active in Women's Rights, author of *Shakespeare's Heroines*.

183 See p. 138 and n. 156.

184 Samuel Gridley Howe (1801–76) and Julia Ward Howe (1819–1910), philanthropist and suffragette. Charlotte Cushman (1816–76) had been in England in 1845–9, 1852, and 1857. She was now embarked on a series of (premature) farewell performances.

185 A romance in hexameters, written in 1849, published in 1858.

186 Eliza Cabot Follen (1787–1860) had married in 1828 Dr Charles Follen. He had died in 1839, leaving also this son, Charles, now 28. James Russell Lowell had written of her: 'And there, too, was Eliza Follen / Who scatters fruit-creating pollen / Where'er a blossom she can find/ Hardy enough for truth's north wind.'

187 Mrs Carolina Maria Seymour Severance (1820–1914), wife of a banker, active in Ohio in Women's Rights. In Boston in 1855 she planned an organization of women for mutual benefit and social work, and later founded the New England Woman's Club.

188 Mrs Maria Weston Chapman (1806–85), wife of Henry Grafton Chapman. At the centre of the Boston Female Antislavery Society, she edited (1836–40) 'Right and Wrong in Boston', the reports of the society. She was, together with Lydia Maria Child and

Lucretia Mott, on the executive committee of the Antislavery Society and was a delegate to the 1840 World Convention.

189 This portion of the entry was apparently written apart, so that Parker's sermon does not read in the proper chronological order as it appears in the diary.

190 BSB's blank.

191 Andrew Jackson Davis (1826–1910) had been 'magnetized' by a local tailor and amateur mesmeric experimenter, which resulted in such 'rare clairvoyance' that the tailor gave up his business to devote his time to Davis and his clairvoyant cures. He made a psychic flight through space, and delivered one hundred and fifty-seven lectures in Manhattan while in a state of trance. They were later published, along with twenty-five other books. His wife was originally Mrs Mary Robinson Love.

192 Parker had delivered a series of sermons to this group of Quakers in Chester County, Pennsylvania on 30–31 May 1858, which he later said were the best things he had written. That appearance and this were among the last sermons Parker delivered. He was already consumptive, and died less than a year later.

193 BSB apparently misunderstood the title of Richard Henry Dana's (1787–1879) book which was, of course, *Two Years Before the Mast*.

194 Sarah Hammond Palfrey, daughter of John Gorham Palfrey, owner and conductor of the *North American Review*.

195 This probably alludes to a painting by Washington Allston (1779–1843), student at the Royal Academy under Benjamin West, friend of Coleridge and Washington Irving, teacher of Samuel F. B. Morse. He returned to America in 1818.

196 Perhaps Sarah Cabot, daughter of Samuel Cabot, who later married Andrew Cunningham Wheelwright, but there were entirely too many prominent Miss Cabots about Boston in the fifties for this to be at all certain.

197 Phillips married Ann Terry Greene in 1837, and she became a nervous invalid shortly thereafter, confined usually to her room and often to her bed.

198 Another of the paintings in the travelling British Exhibition.

ASHWORTH, HENRY, *A Tour in the United States, Cuba, and Canada* (London: A. W. Bennett, 1861); visited 1856.

BARCLAY-ALLARDICE, ROBERT, *Agricultural Tour in the United States and Upper Canada* (Edinburgh: William Blackwood & Sons, 1842); visited 1841.

BISHOP, MRS ISABELLA LUCY BIRD, *The Englishwoman in America* (London: John Murray, 1856).

BREMER, FREDRIKA, *America of the Fifties: Letters of Fredrika Bremer* (Homes of the New World, Impressions of America, trans. by Mary Howitt, 2 volumes, Harper & Bros, New York 1853; reprinted, selected and edited by Adolph B. Benson, American Scandinavian Foundation, New York, 1924); visited 1849. She is not English, but included here because of BSB's allusion to her.

COBDEN, RICHARD, *The American Diaries*, edited, with an introduction and notes, by Elizabeth Hoon Cowley (Princeton University Press, 1952); visited 1835, 1859.

CUNYNGHAME, LT-COL. ARTHUR, *A Glimpse at the Great Western Republic* (London: Richard Bentley, 1851).

DAVIES, EBENEZER, *American Scenes and Christian Slavery* (London: John Snow, 1849).

DICKENS, CHARLES, *American Notes for General Circulation* (London: Chapman and Hall, 1842).

EVEREST, REV. ROBERT, *A Journey through the U.S. and Part of Canada* (London: J. Chapman, 1855).

FINCH, MARIANNE, *An Englishwoman's Experience in America* (London: Richard Bentley, 1853).

GODLEY, JOHN ROBERT, *Letters from America* (London: John Murray, 1844, 2 vols); visited 1842.

GRATTAN, THOMAS COLLEY, *Civilized America* (London: Bradbury & Evans, 1859); visited 1839, 1845.

LEWIS, THE REV. GEORGE, *Impressions of America and the American Churches* (Edinburgh: Kennedy, 1845); visited 1844.

LYELL, SIR CHARLES, *A Second Visit to the United States of North America* (New York: Harper & Bros., 1850, 2 vols); visited 1845.

MACKAY, ALEXANDER, *The Western World; or Travels in the United States in 1846-1847* (Philadelphia: Lea & Blanchard, 1849).

MACKAY, CHARLES, *Life and Liberty in America* (London, Smith, Elder & Co., 1859, 2 vols); visited 1857.

MURRAY, THE HON. AMELIA M., *Letters from the United States, Cuba, and Canada* (New York: G. P. Putnam & Co., 1856); visited 1854.

PULSZKY, FRANCIS and THERESA, *White, Red, Black* (New York: Redfield, 1853); not English but Hungarian; writing for the English audience; they accompanied Kossuth to the States.

REDPATH, JAMES, *The Roving Editor* (New York, 1859).

STURGE, JOSEPH, *A Visit to the United States in 1841* (Boston: Dexter S. King, 1842).

TROLLOPE, ANTHONY, *North America* (New York: Harper & Bros., 1862).

WHIPPLE, HENRY BENJAMIN, *Bishop Whipple's Southern Diary, 1834–1844*, edited, with an introduction by Lester B. Shippee (Minneapolis: University of Minnesota Press, 1937).

Bodichon—*cont.*

discouragement 49; family 37; illegitimacy 37, 46; finances 44, 50, 52; friends 39–44, 47, 48–9; health 33–4, 51–3; independence 45; opinionated 31–2 life 30–53; activism 26; goes to lectures 4; liaison with Chapman 32–7; sent to Algeria 37; marriage 30; causes misgivings 38; wedding trip 25; travel plans 689

American travels 38–9

describes: Alabama 118; Alabama River 112; countryside around Savannah 122; countryside north of Wilmington 132; St Lawrence River 148; Savannah River 127–8; Vermont 153–4; woods 74–5

discusses: America's moral state 94; divorce 86; fashions 87; on *Baltic* 61; slavery 97; cruelty to slaves 100–2

lists things to bring home from America 113–14

opinions of: America 26, 129; Americans 133; American art 103; American churches 138–9; American fauna 124; American freedom 72; American horses 145; American liberty and audacity 129; children 113; death 109; steamboats 57; Amelia M. Murray 25; New Orleans 111; the right to vote 73; Savannah 121; slavery 61–3, 97–9, 120, 123–4, 130–1; books about slavery 99; snakes 121; spiritualism 46; tyranny in Europe 153

sees: Mason-Dixon line 136; Peale's *Court of Death* 103

sends seeds 136; takes nature walk 64

visits: astrologer 96; churches 69; African Baptist 119; Baptist 105–7, 125; black churches 83–4, 87; Church of the Divine Humanity 82; Methodist 107–8, 125; Presbyterian 138; Unitarian 137–8; visits falls of the Montmorency River 153; Niagara 144–6, 152; female M.D.s 94; R. W. Emerson 161; graveyard in New Orleans 69; Lyceum 84; medium 110; Lucretia Mott 139–41; Music Hall in Boston 158; Raritan Bay Union 142–4; schools: 91; black 88–90; Franklin School 99–100; girls' school 97; slave auction 103; slave cabin 65; White House 136

residence: Mobile 110; New Orleans 66, 71; Boston 123

her causes: afforestation and sanitation in Algeria 49; a petition 47; experiments in primary education 48; Women's Rights 39, 42, 134; university education for women 49; admission of women to university examinations 50; Girton College 50–1

her writings: 48; Chapman's advice 35; *A Brief Summary, in Plain Language, of the Most Important Laws Concerning Women* 47; *Objections to the Enfranchisement of Women Considered* 48; *Reasons for the Enfranchisement of Women* 48; *Women at Work* 48; journals 27

her drawings and paintings: 43–5; Chapman to show, 35; sketch of goat 80, of river town 59, of alligator

INDEX